Please ensure this item is
returned on or before the

Latest Date Due

stamped on this slip.

Carter .

2 4 MAR 200
Blair
1 2 MAY 200
Vinling
Sedgman
JOYNER
Heath 2/08
Abel Tasman 8/08
Montgomerie 01.09
BALF 11/10
MOGFORD)

Stendt
BOSTROM

Space below is for your personal mark

JULIE CHRISTIE

JULIE CHRISTIE

Anthony Hayward

Chivers Press   Thorndike Press
Bath, England ● Thorndike, Maine USA

This Large Print edition is published by Chivers Press, England, and by Thorndike Press, USA.

Published in 2001 in the U.K. by arrangement with Robert Hale Limited.

Published in 2001 in the U.S. by arrangement with Robert Hale Limited.

U.K. Hardcover ISBN 0–7540–4424–6   (Chivers Large Print)
U.S. Softcover   ISBN 0–7862–3189–0   (General Series Edition)

The text of this Large Print edition is unabridged.
Other aspects of the book may vary from the original edition.

Set in 16 pt. New Times Roman.

Printed in Great Britain on acid-free paper.

British Library Cataloguing in Publication Data available

Library of Congress Cataloging-in-Publication Data

Hayward, Anthony.
  Julie Christie / Anthony Hayward.
      p.   cm.
  Originally published: London : Robert Hale, 2000.
  ISBN 0–7862–3189–0 (lg. print : sc : alk. paper)
  1. Christie, Julie. 2. Motion picture actors and actresses—
  Great Britain—Biography. 3. Large type books. I. Title.
  PN2598.C37 H39 2001
  791.43'028'092—dc21
    [B]   00–066661

CONTENTS

ACKNOWLEDGEMENTS

Many people and organizations have helped with my research for this biography. I would like to thank staff at the British Film Institute National Library and Special Collections department, London; the Theatre Museum, London; the British Library's Oriental and India Office Collections Reading Room, London; the British Library Newspaper Library, London; the Shakespeare Centre Library, Stratford-upon-Avon; Birmingham Central Library; Leeds Central Library; the Family Records Centre, London; and the Probate Search Room, London, and the Probate Registry, York.

For their memories of working with Julie Christie, quoted and unquoted, and in some cases for help in finding information and contacts, I am grateful to John Altman, Ken Annakin, Bernard Archard, Raymond Baxter, Ann Beach, Rodney Bewes, Joyce Blair, John Box, Richard Briers, Kate Campbell, Phyllis Dalton, Pauline Delany, Tracey Eddon, Gerry Fisher, Michael Fleming, Harry Fowler, David Gladwell, Nickolas Grace, Alec Guinness, Michael Hayes, Roger Howells, Pauline Jameson, Freddie Jones, Jeremy Kemp, Barbara Lane, Jamie Leonard, Richard Lester, Ian Lewis, Roger Lloyd Pack, Leonie Mellinger, John Nettleton, Roger Randall-

Cutler, Brian Rawlinson, Nicolas Roeg, Clifford Rose, Allan Scott, William Simons, Marianne Stone, Alex Thomson, Richard Thorp, Frederick Treves, Derek Ware, Tom Watson, Paul Weston, Ronald Wilson, Anna Wing and Peter Wood.

Thanks also to Doreen Haigh, Elsie White, Sister Stephanie of the Convent of Our Lady, St Leonard's-on-Sea, Albert Evans of the Central School of Speech and Drama, Iris Henson, treasurer of the Friends of Frinton Theatre, Betty and Iris Bessant, and John Hiscock and Douglas Thompson, as well as to Michael Cook for translation of French magazine features. Thanks, as always, to Deborah.

INTRODUCTION

Staying on in India during the summer of 1982, Julie Christie bade farewell to the cast and crew that had just filmed *Heat and Dust* with her in Hyderabad and set out on a voyage of rediscovery. That country and the last days of the Raj formed the actress's earliest memories from the time when her father managed tea plantations in the Assam region. On her return, forty-two years after her birth there, Christie went barefoot, donned a cotton skirt and T-shirt, and sought to find out something about the land that she had never understood in seven years as a child.

With filming over, she ventured into the Himalayas with her boyfriend, Duncan Campbell, and savoured the mystical qualities of India in the mountain range that connects Assam to the rest of the country. 'I love India so much,' she explained. 'I have never had this reaction to a place before and, at the moment, I can't put my feelings into words.' Whether affected by a return to her roots or simply by the discovery of this tantalizing land, the actress was clearly moved.

The 1980s was a time of reassessment for Christie. After two decades of international fame, she decided to step back, retreat to her Welsh cottage and accept only roles that she found interesting or in line with her social and political beliefs. Critics found it strange that someone whose beauty and presence had made her an icon of the 1960s should shun mainstream cinema and vocalize her concerns for humanity. But Christie proved genuine in her beliefs, spending much time on issues such as nuclear disarmament, animal welfare and American aggression towards Nicaragua.

Christie's spellbinding presence had certainly made her a true spirit of the Swinging Sixties, in films such as *Billy Liar!*, *Darling*, *Doctor Zhivago* and *Far from the Madding Crowd*, and in the 1970s she had made notable films such as *The Go-Between*, *McCabe & Mrs Miller* and *'Don't Look Now'*. However, from very early on in her career, which was punctuated by lengthy breaks away from the screen, Christie had chosen her film roles carefully, often influenced by who was directing.

'As an actress, my ambition is always to have the best directors,' she said. 'I am a great film fan and I love working with the great ones, such as John Schlesinger, David Lean and François Truffaut. Working with them is like being a student of art working with the old masters.' Christie also acted in films made by Richard Lester, Joseph Losey, Robert Altman, James Ivory and Sidney Lumet, and had a relationship with American actor Warren Beatty, which coincided with a move to

Hollywood that would have been natural for most high-flying British actresses.

But, after ten years in the world's film capital and no longer with Beatty, Christie returned to Britain, settled in Wales and was seen on screen in mostly low-budget independent films. By the mid 1990s, she had returned to mainstream cinema, acting in the medieval fantasy *DragonHeart* and Kenneth Branagh's epic version of *Hamlet*, before securing her third Oscar nomination in 1998 for *Afterglow*. But, even then, she denied that this signalled a comeback. One of British cinema's most charismatic stars remained an enigma, appearing to have no thirst for the medium that had made her a worldwide star. Fame meant nothing to Christie, and she could not be persuaded to do anything for which she had no desire.

CHAPTER ONE

A COSMOPOLITAN CHILDHOOD

The last days of British colonialism in India provided the first childhood experiences for Julie Christie. Overseeing the 'natives' presented young Englishmen with a potentially good career, and her father, Francis St John Christie, had found his opportunity in the tea business. In the mid 1920s, at about the time that E.M. Forster's novel *A Passage to India* was accused of stirring up anti-imperialism and betraying the British 'cause' there, Francis started work in the plantations of Assam, the north-eastern province of plains and river valleys where more than half of India's tea was grown.

Frank's own father, George Francis Stephen Christie, had already enjoyed a distinguished career as a civil servant in the colonial administrations of India and Burma, which the British ruled as a province of the jewel in their imperial crown. In several areas of Burma, George Christie served as district commissioner and divisional and session judge, the highest-ranking local government official. He was also important enough to be one of three British officials to write a report on the nearby Cocos Islands after complaints from

Indians there about their conditions and pay. After visiting the islands, he declared that the inhabitants 'expressed themselves as thoroughly satisfied with their life and treatment', although the dissenters had actually been removed to Calcutta before his trip.

George's son, Frank, who had two sisters, was in his early twenties when he started working for the large, London-based Jokai (Assam) Tea Company. He stepped up the ladder from being an assistant at the firm's Tippuk, Pathalipam, Woodbine and Nalam divisions to manage plantations in Nokhroy and Lengrai, before marrying Rosemary Ramsden. His wife came from an English family who had long been in the Indian tea business. Though originally from Yorkshire, they moved to Hove, East Sussex, where Rosemary lived before her marriage. Her father, George, was by then a director of the Doom-Dooma Tea Company, another big English firm with plantations in Assam, after working his way up from being an assistant and manager for Jokai in the 1890s to superintendent at the Pabbojan Tea Company.

Rosemary's mother, Margaret, was from the Scottish Hannay family of Indian tea planters, with ancestors who had served in the Gurkhas and the Indian Navy. 'Maggie', as she was known, had experienced the tragedy of seeing another daughter, also named Margaret, die at the age of eight months in April 1900, after contracting dysentery. She gave birth to son John eight years later and daughter Rosemary in 1912. With their children grown up, the Ramsdens had a double celebration in 1937, when Rosemary married Frank Christie in September and John, who was continuing the family tradition by working in the teaplanting business, wed Betty Bundock two months later. Both ceremonies took place at the Anglican St John's Church, in Calcutta.

At that time, Frank Christie managed Jokai's Singlijan division, based at Lahoal, in the Lakhimpur district of Assam, in the far north-eastern corner of the province, near the border with Tibet. It was there that their daughter, Julie Frances, was born on 14 April 1940, and three months later she was baptized at St Paul's Church, Dibrugarh.

Although Assam was an isolated region, connected to the rest of India only by a narrow corridor through the Himalayas, the Christies were part of the huge British community in the subcontinent, comprising soldiers and government officials, businessmen, doctors, nurses, engineers, surveyors, journalists and teachers, missionaries and governesses. Like Frank Christie, all of these people were trying to make careers for themselves in a mystical land where they experienced extremes of climate that would cause them to sweat in the heat at the same time as getting soaked by the rain. Assam, however, escapes the hot, dry season and is prey to the highest rainfall in the country, often resulting in flooding.

Some expatriates were from several generations of families whose Indian connections went back to the time of the British East India Company, which in the seventeenth century had been granted a charter by Elizabeth I to supply Asian spices and peppers to Europe. The company controlled India until the British government took over rule of the country in 1858 after a massacre of British officers and residents by native Indian soldiers. One of Rosemary Christie's ancestors had been a colonel in the Gurkhas during the mutiny. In the years that followed, Indian independence movements sprang up to demand self-rule.

The attractions of India for Britons such as Frank and Rosemary Christie were evident. The cost of living was low and there was almost no income tax, so the lifestyle was ideal for a father bringing up a family. Wives and children would have little contact with Indians, except servants such as an *ayah*—a nanny or nurse. An official report in the 1940s concluded that tea-plantation labourers were paid too little and that more should be done to improve education and sanitation facilities. The British were providing jobs for the natives, but the gap between the imperial bosses and the workers in their own country

4

highlighted the differences between the rulers and the ruled. This was the sort of injustice against which Julie Christie would campaign less than half a century later.

But the Victorian and Edwardian atmosphere invoked by the British in India before independence seemed a million miles away from the realities of the modern world that many had left back home. As the Germans were sweeping through Europe towards Britain during the first half of 1940, Frank and Rosemary Christie were getting to grips with parenthood, after daughter Julie's birth. However, they were not immune to the Second World War hostilities. Assam was used as one of the main supply routes for Allied troops to gain access to neighbouring Burma, where they finally defeated the Japanese after the seizure of that country in 1942. During this time, parts of Assam were bombed by the Japanese and battles fought there stopped that country's army advancing into India.

When film fame came in the mid 1960s, Christie had no tales of war to tell but satisfied interviewers' desires for information about her young days by regaling them with stories of her clashes with authority. 'When I was naughty,' she explained, 'my Indian *ayah* took me out and tied me to a tree with a leather belt. "The tigers will come and get you," she said. It was very dark and I strained against the leather and I screamed. I was out there, I suppose, for five minutes and there wasn't any real danger, but I have never forgotten it. Never. She was an old cow, that *ayah*.'

Such was life for the children of those English who helped to uphold colonial rule during the last days of the Raj. In her older, more politically aware days, Christie—whose family was steeped in colonialism—claimed not to remember about her time in India. The actress showed an increasing tendency towards forgetfulness in all aspects of her life as she aged, even finding it difficult to recall details of her early films. In the 1980s, Christie likened imperialism to the way in which human beings treated animals and considered themselves to be better. 'I know it's a very common human reaction to anything that is "different", paralleling the disdain of colonials for the "difference" of the people of their colonies,' she said.

After the First World War, Indian nationalism had gained pace and unrest accompanied the campaign of civil disobedience launched by Mahatma Gandhi and his Congress Party. Moves to give some degree of autonomy in the Indian provinces failed to satisfy nationalist leaders, and the Second World War only delayed the inevitable.

The young Christie's last couple of years in India, which was divided between two great religious communities, the Hindus and Muslims, were a turbulent time. In 1946 the post-war British Labour government offered independence to the whole of the country, but the Muslim minority would not agree to be governed by the Hindu majority, with the result that rioting broke out.

Eventually, the British agreed to the Muslims' calls for partition, and in August 1947, overseen by Lord Mountbatten, Britain's last Viceroy and Governor-General of India, the Hindu lands became an independent India and the Muslim-dominated areas became the new state of East and West Pakistan, with its own government. However, the violence was not over, for tens of millions of Hindus and Muslims left in the 'wrong' country had to flee from their homes and many were massacred by their historical adversaries.

Despite the bloodshed, some of the British, especially those with business interests, stayed on in India. They included Frank Christie, who continued his career with the Jokai tea company by moving to its Koilamari division as manager. Others who saw a future there included Geoffrey Kendal and his actress wife Laura Liddell, who toured the country in a travelling Shakespearean theatre company in which their daughter Felicity made her stage debut in 1947, at the age of nine months, in *A Midsummer Night's Dream*. The family's adventures were later immortalized in Ismail Merchant and James Ivory's evocative 1965 film *Shakespeare Wallah* and Felicity went on to find success on the British stage and in television. Christie herself would later act in the producer-director partnership's film *Heat and Dust*, also set in India.

However, shortly before partition, Frank and Rosemary Christie, who by then also had a young son, Clive, decided that their daughter should leave India to be educated in England. Rosemary took the seven-year-old back to Sussex and advertised for an 'auntie' to look after her, before returning to her husband on the tea plantation. 'Suddenly, there were no servants, it was cold, I couldn't walk around barefoot,' said Christie later. 'The little things that made up the fabric of the first six years of my life were suddenly ripped away.'

While attending a day school in Bexhill, the seven-year-old lived with a retired couple in the town, but she was later enrolled in boarding schools. 'The woman was a most wonderful person,' Christie recalled of her 'Auntie Elsie'. 'I was very, very happy with her and loved her very much. She was very different from my mother, and I was lucky to have both their influences on me.' When Christie switched to a boarding school, she turned the loneliness to her advantage. 'During holidays, I had to stay at school, sometimes with only one other girl,' she recalled. 'It made me very independent. I loved it. I learned to get along without my parents, without anybody.'

The separation from her mother and father had an effect on Christie, though. 'I was loved by everyone, but it wasn't much good because my parents weren't with me,' she explained. 'My mother was the most important person in my life, but we were two strong-willed women and had our fights. She should have been an academic but was a wife and mother because of that generation.'

Christie's mother moved back to Britain with son Clive in 1950, after a huge earthquake in Assam that year, which caused heavy landslides and great flooding. Rosemary and Frank's marriage was under strain and the tea planter visited his wife and family on only a handful of occasions at their new home, a three-bedroom converted oast house in the East Sussex hamlet of Gun Hill, near Horam. The couple's personalities were different enough to cause friction. 'Frank was a bit on the highly strung side,' recalled family friend Doreen Haigh, whose husband, John, worked on the same tea plantation as Christie's father. 'He used to have strong reactions, whereas Rosemary was very intelligent and had complete control of whatever she said and did. Frank was on the excitable side, and the two didn't go together very well. Rosemary was very clever and a bit above him academically.'

But the darkest cloud hanging over the marriage was the existence of Frank's illegitimate daughter, born to an Indian before he married Rosemary. June Christie's birth was one that might have brought shame on Frank's subsequent family, but it was not unusual among the British community in India. 'In tea planting, parents who were particular about their children never left them there to be educated,' explained Doreen Haigh.

Children had to come to England and wives had to come also to establish them. This caused trouble because, when they left, it was a case of six months away. In that time, married tea planters always had Indian mistresses, as did bachelors. These Indian mistresses were really approved by their firms—it was just one of those things. They were very young, very attractive and usually in their early twenties. Of course, the tea planters lived with these girls and had children by these girls. Even the unmarried ones did so.

Although many of these children were sent to a school in Kalinpong, even further into Upper Assam, where there was snow, June was educated at a mission school in Dibrugarh. 'This little girl was extremely clever and she had two sisters,' said Doreen Haigh. 'Those two sisters were not very strong and they both died. This clever one stayed with my husband while Frank came to England to try and sort things out with Rosemary.'

The marriage collapsed and Rosemary brought up her two children alone in Sussex. 'She didn't have a job, but she obviously had money and enjoyed gardening,' said Elsie White, the family's cleaner. 'In those days, there were the upper class and the lower class, but Rosemary got on with people whatever class they were in. Frank had a black girl out in India, but Rosemary never talked about her much. Julie was a very happy-go-lucky girl. She and Clive used to play with my two boys, Colin and Leslie. I remember them playing an old Sussex game called stoolball.'

Julie Christie's secondary education was a tale of moving from one school to another. From the age of eleven, she was a pupil at a convent and gained a reputation for being extrovert. 'I went to a variety of schools and at all of them I was never particularly popular at first,' she explained. 'They called me S.O., which means Show Off, and I suppose I was. I was an obnoxious child. I used to make up stories which made me the heroine . . . how I strangled the python when it attacked our beaver in India. None of it was true. I don't think I ever saw a snake. I suppose it was because I was terribly shy as a child—in some ways I still am—and, to cover it up, I behaved as I did.'

According to her mother, the young Christie was fond of dressing up and acted in school plays. 'The only times I wasn't shy was when I was on stage,' said the actress. 'I went to a convent school for a while, although now I am not particularly religious. I was expelled from that for telling dirty stories. They weren't particularly terrible—no worse than any child tells around twelve—but one of the other girls' mothers threatened to take her daughter away unless I was expelled, So the nuns expelled me. They were wrong to give in like that. Then, late, I took my O-levels and I was good at history and English, but I failed in French.'

Christie boarded at the Convent of Our Lady, St Leonard's-on-Sea, from January 1952 until December 1953, after leaving St Francis School, Bexhill, and her name appeared regularly in the nuns' weekly report book. Among the many comments recorded were: 'Julie's hair was untidy'; 'Julie caught giving note to Rosemary King to send to a mutual school friend'; 'Julie Christie disrespectful—asked to show her brushes, she said, "*Here* you are!"'; 'Julie Christie untidy desk and dirty tunic'; 'Noisy and bad-mannered in the refectory'; 'Late for mass'; 'Julie Christie has not given in her Latin written work three times'; 'Late for breakfast'; 'Julie Christie continually being pulled up for interrupting'; 'Impertinence in class'; 'Very late for evening prayers twice'; 'Disobedient at recreation and in dormitory'; 'Talking in the dormitory at 11.30'; and 'Left recreation without permission'.

Diana Brinkworth was a friend and regular cohort in Christie's antics. They shared a dormitory with Katey Twomey, Pat Fitzpatrick, Amanda Murray-Lewis and Rosamund Aiton, who went on to become a professional pianist. Sister Stephanie, who joined the school, now closed, as a teacher during Christie's time there, recalled:

Julie was so vital, she would have made a good friend to any child. She was an extrovert, lively girl—vividly alive, full of life and exciting—but she was very naughty according to the standards of those days, which were very different from today. It was just mischief, really. I think it was pretty awful that she was considered a naughty girl for such little things, but people were very stuffy then. I didn't teach Julie, but I supervised her at games and my greatest memory of her is crossing the games field with her and, instead of walking across, she was circling around and jumping the whole time.

Rosemary Christie, getting used to life in Sussex without her husband, was devastated by her daughter's expulsion. 'I met her mother on that particular day,' recalled Doreen Haigh. 'I visited her with my husband and she said, "Oh, Dodo," which was my pet name, "Julie has

13

been expelled from school and we're so upset about it." I said, "Now don't worry about it—these are all the problems of growing up." ' At a subsequent day school, Christie was in trouble again for exciting the boys by tucking her dress into her knickers.

Then, at a boarding school in High Wycombe, Buckinghamshire, she took her seven O-levels at the age of sixteen, at a time when most children in Britain finished their last year of compulsory education aged fifteen. Once the teenager had taken her exams, Rosemary Christie decided that her daughter needed a break and thought she might improve her grasp of French by going to live in that country. So Christie stayed with a large, rather eccentric but intellectual family in Tarbes, Gascony, in south-west France, gaining a basic command of the language and developing an interest in art. The father was writing a dictionary of the Basque language.

'Not many people have heard of the place,' said Christie. 'It's right down in the Pyrenees and certainly no one spoke English, which meant I *had* to get on with the job of learning French. I have always wanted to act, but I think it is essential to know another language, if only to be able to read a book in its original language. A translation is never the same.'

The sight of the family flying into rages with each other was a contrast to the English restraint with which Christie had grown up.

Although unhappy and homesick at first, she settled down and enjoyed the social life of dances, parties and boys. During her year there, she discovered a freedom and independence that was to shape her outlook on life after such an unsettled childhood.

Journalist David Lewin, given the privilege of looking through Christie's photograph album with her in 1965, noted that the pictures before and after her time in France revealed the transformation from 'a gawky little child with light-brown hair and not particularly attractive features' to a young woman, 'taller, the figure fuller, the hair lighter' and hints of the smile that was to become familiar to audiences worldwide. However, Christie's shyness had not been overcome and her highly strung disposition stayed with her, making her nervous of meeting new people. She also claimed to be lazy, a trait that she still confessed to in the 1990s as she made a return to mainstream cinema after spending years in the wilderness.

After her time in France, Christie travelled back to Sussex and enrolled to take A-levels at Brighton Technical College. 'I went there for a while but didn't learn very much,' she said. 'I do remember drinking a lot of coffee in many coffee-houses. And the poetry of Gerard Manley Hopkins.'

Changing her mind about a career in art, she decided that acting was what she wanted to do. So, at the age of eighteen, Christie successfully auditioned at the Central School of Speech and Drama, in London, although her father's apparent prosperity meant that she did not qualify for a grant. Living on little money, she bought an airbed and begged space on friends' floors for a while. Despite the nomadic existence, Christie was doing what she wanted to do and developing the independence that had flourished in childhood, although at the same time growing to value friends. That combination of independence of mind and being surrounded by others was something that would continue through her life.

She also developed a new outlook towards people. 'I grew up conservative—I was a real snob,' she said. 'Even at 19 the idea of going out with someone with any sort of accent was intolerable, disgusting. Then I went to London, to drama school, and found a boyfriend with a very broad cockney accent, so all those assumptions changed.'

CHAPTER TWO

PLUCKED FROM OBSCURITY

Christie made an immediate impact at the Central School of Speech and Drama. Jeremy Kemp, who went on to play PC Bob Steele in the early days of the television police series *Z Cars*, before moving into films, was in his final year there at the time she started. 'When my year were doing a production that was being watched by agents and directors, the first-year students acted as ushers,' recalled Kemp. 'They were being generally helpful and smiled and gave people a programme.'

On this occasion, Julie was undertaking that task. Afterwards, I met the agent Philip Pearman, who was also the actress Coral Browne's first husband. He asked me, 'Who was that delicious little creature who was disseminating literature at the door?' I replied, 'I have no difficulty in guessing who it might be. Her name is Julie Christie and I would put my money on her being a movie star.' I remember that she was notably attractive, vivacious, mildly extrovert and nice to have around.

During her course, Christie also made an

impression on another visitor to Central. Peter Hoar, who ran Frinton Summer Theatre, in Essex, with his brother, Sam, and sister-in-law, Joan Shore, invited her to join their repertory company during the holiday. The small Frinton Theatre's summer seasons had launched stars such as Michael Denison, Vanessa Redgrave and Roger Moore on to the ladder of success. The company performed a different play each week, running from Thursday to Wednesday, which allowed holidaymakers to see at least two productions during their stay in the English east coast seaside town.

Christie was seen at Frinton Summer Theatre in 1960, most notably playing Michael Fleming's girlfriend in the comedy *Two Little Bustleworms*, the story of a young scientific research doctor who has little time for women until he discovers that even bustleworms go in pairs. 'The play was a load of old crap,' recalled Fleming, 'but Julie looked a million dollars and had a sort of élan.' Two other young actresses who performed in the same season at Frinton were Jane Asher and Suzanne Neve.

During Christie's final year at the Central School of Speech and Drama, she starred in the title role of an end-of-term production of *The Diary of Anne Frank* that was to have a significant effect on her career. Among those in the audience was television producer

18

Michael Hayes, who had directed the BBC's acclaimed 1960 series *An Age of Kings*, which ran Shakespeare's plays together to cover eighty-six years of English history and the lives of seven monarchs. Also there watching were British-based Italian film producer Joseph Janni, and director John Schlesinger, who had already made a film called *The Class* for the BBC arts series *Monitor* in April 1961, in which acting coach Harold Lang was seen giving Central drama students a lesson in improvisation.

Christie, then a third-year student, did not feature in the *Monitor* programme, but Schlesinger—who subsequently switched to making televison dramas before becoming one of Britain's most successful film directors—saw her in the *Anne Frank* production. He considered the aspiring actress to be 'not terribly talented in that particular role'. Although Janni later declared himself to be impressed by her performance, Christie claimed that the producer had hardly noticed her, failing to recognize the acting student when they passed on a staircase afterwards.

However, during her last term at drama school, Christie went to audition in front of the two men when they teamed up to make *A Kind of Loving*, a gritty screen version of Stan Barstow's novel about a young couple forced into a shotgun marriage when the teenaged girl becomes pregnant. It was one of the new breed of socio-realistic films being made in Britain in the late 1950s and early 1960s, hot on the heels of books and stage plays that reflected working-class culture for the first time. However, Christie did not get a part in *A Kind of Loving*, Janni considering her 'too exciting' and not right for the film, which eventually starred Alan Bates and June Ritchie, and won great acclaim. On leaving drama school, Christie performed in another repertory summer season in Frinton, then landed a television role that put her face in households throughout Britain and alerted film producers and directors to her star quality. Michael Hayes, the BBC television producer-director who had watched the actress in *The Diary of Anne Frank* at Central, picked Christie to play the android of the title role in the 1961 futuristic serial *A for Andromeda*. It was the first attempt by television at serious, adult-orientated science fiction since writer Nigel Kneale's three *Quatermass* serials of the 1950s had held the nation spellbound—and terrified—with their stories of alien threats to Earth.

When I was casting *A for Andromeda*, I happened to be speaking to an agent over a drink who said he had seen this girl at Central who he thought was very good, [recalled Hayes]. He talked of her in terms of being another Brigitte Bardot. So I went to see Julie in *The Diary of Anne Frank*, in which she was wearing a dark wig. Afterwards, I met her and she seemed extremely right for the role. It was basically her appearance, to be honest, but she also had no problem acting and was very good as Anne Frank.

The new drama, in seven, 45-minute episodes, was conceived by novelist Fred Hoyle, who was professor of astronomy and experimental philosophy at Cambridge University, and scripted by BBC producer John Elliot, who went on to produce the boardroom-to-bedroom drama *Mogul* and its sequel, *The Troubleshooters. A for Andromeda* was based on Hoyle's premise that man's first contact with an alien civilization would come through radio-astronomy.

So the serial, set in 1970, began with signals from the fictional Andromeda galaxy in outer space being received by a powerful, new radio telescope high in the Yorkshire Dales. Idealistic young scientist Dr John Fleming decodes them to discover that they are instructions for building a computer that can generate human life. Fleming's colleague, biologist Madeleine Dawnay (played by Mary Morris), uses the information to experiment in manufacturing a living organism.

Although not seen in the first episode, Christie subsequently played brunette lab assistant Christine, who is fatally electrocuted by the computer and, as a result of Dawnay's experiment in creating a human embryo, is reborn as an exquisite blonde replica, christened Andromeda. She has a mental link with the computer and induces it to design a new missile system for the government. Fleming, played by Peter Halliday, realizes that the computer's control over Andromeda is a menace and eventually persuades her that it should be destroyed. As Andromeda in the final three episodes, Christie does not speak at first but is gradually taught to do so.

Other stars of the serial included Esmond Knight, a film star and classical stage actor; Frank Windsor, who subsequently found fame as police detective John Watt in *Z Cars* and *Softly Softly*; Jack May, by then already known on radio as Nelson Gabriel in *The Archers* and later to play the valet Simms alongside Gerald Harper in another 1960s fantasy series, *Adam Adamant Lives!*; and stage actress Patricia Kneale.

Although there was some location filming in Pembrokeshire, most of the serial was made at the BBC's White City studios, in West London, not far from Christie's flat. Once again, Christie made a great impresson on those with whom she worked. John Nettleton, who acted security man Harries, recalled her arriving on the set as 'a stunningly pretty girl' and Frederick Treves, taking the role of naval officer Captain Lovell in Christie's first episode, formed a close bond with her during the filming. 'She was very charming, amusing and laidback,' he said. 'To me, she was like Richard Burton. Both had an indescribable quality, a charisma that put them aside of others. She was also quite innocent, not in a naïve way, but she was trusting of people. It was a very positive thing of being a good person.'

Off screen, Treves discovered that Christie was experiencing difficulties in her love-life. 'I used to drive Julie home to her flat in Notting Hill,' said Treves. 'She had a strange boyfriend who was very jealous and could be rather aggressive. She told me that he got a knife and tore her clothes to pieces.'

On screen, Christie had no such problems. *A for Andromeda*, transmitted in the autumn of 1961, became an early classic of science-fiction television and the final episode was watched by 5.4 million households, making it one of the most popular programmes of the time. It gave Christie her screen break but, by the time a sequel, *The Andromeda Breakthrough*, was made two years later, she had moved into feature films and Susan Hampshire took over the title role.

The BBC had not moved quickly enough to sign her for another series. 'After the final episode of the first series was made,' recalled producer Michael Hayes, 'I was walking to a drinks reception at Television Centre and met the BBC's controller of programmes on the way. I said to him, "Sign this girl up now. I don't take great credit for spotting stars but, if you don't get her, you're stuffed for a sequel." Needless to say, nothing was done and they lost her.'

Christie was, in fact, seen on television in a different series just two days before her first appearance in *A for Andromeda* was broadcast. Having recorded the science-fiction serial, she acted a patient in an episode of *Call Oxbridge 2000*, a spin-off from the popular hospital series *Emergency—Ward 30*, transmitted live on ITV on Sunday afternoons. In this episode, Dr John Rennie was called out when three girls at an exclusive finishing school complained of sore throats and feeling unwell—a day before their exams. Suzanne Neve, who had acted at Frinton Summer Theatre during Christie's first season there, also appeared. Richard Thorp, who starred as Dr Rennie and has since become known to millions of viewers as Alan Turner in *Emmerdale*, was struck by Christie's screen presence. 'She was drop-dead gorgeous and the camera absolutely adored her,' he said. 'I just thought, this lady is going to make it.'

A star-in-the-making who shared this admiration for Christie was Terence Stamp, who would later team up with her in *Far from the Madding Crowd*. The young actor had just filmed his soon-to-be-acclaimed role in Peter Ustinov's screen version of *Billy Budd* when he spotted a photograph of Christie on the cover of a new magazine, *Town*, taken by Terence Donovan and showing her dressed in an open blue denim shirt and holding a Sten gun. He showed it to his flatmate Michael Caine, who had just returned from making *Zulu* in South Africa—a couple of bachelor boys looking for fun and females. 'I know her,' Caine said, instantly, explaining that he had met her in the BBC canteen while she was making *A for Andromeda* and he was rehearsing a television play. Caine recalled later:

I collected my meal and was about to join some actors whom I knew vaguely, when I spotted this girl seated alone at a table in the corner. She was stunning. She was so stunning that she had actually frightened everybody off. I had no scruples and went straight over and asked her, rather unnecessarily I thought, if the other nine empty seats at her table were taken. She informed me with a toe-curling smile that they were not, and invited me to sit down . . . After our first meeting I quickly realized that there was nothing here for me romantically but she was nice and I liked her. I saw her around many times after that and we knew each other as vague friends.

Stamp demanded that Caine put him in touch with Christie, but his friend did not have her telephone number. Determined to meet her, Stamp went to the trendy new Discotheque club in Wardour Street, centre of the film industry's distribution companies and post-production work. He saw Christine Keeler, subsequently to become notorious in the Profumo Affair, but not Christie. Later, actor-writer Derek Marlow visited Stamp and Caine's flat in Ebury Street, just north of the Thames, and mentioned that he knew Christie. He agreed to introduce her to Stamp and eventually arranged a blind date in the West End, at the Seven Stars restaurant in the Coventry Street Corner House.

The differences in Stamp and Christie's characters were apparent when they arrived there, he overdressing and donning a loosely worn gold bracelet watch, she being shy and not very talkative. However, Christie did declare during the meal that she had always wanted a rocking chair, and after agreeing to another date, at the new Casserole restaurant in the King's Road, Chelsea, Stamp arranged for Harrod's to deliver a wooden one while they were eating. She was delighted and the pair's romance proceeded apace, despite the imbalance that she was from a well-off family but had no interest in materialism, while he was the son of two cockneys and was happy to lap up all the perks of being an up-and-coming actor.

'To me she will always be a bohemian from the Fifties,' Stamp later reflected of Christie. 'She had little or no regard for the trappings and finery I sought to bolster up my success, and when I first saw where she lived I was taken aback by the proportions of her little room, with its broken window through which stray cats crawled. I had shared flats all my student days, still did, but Julie's lifestyle was a forerunner of the hippy communes.'

Christie's retiring nature came to the fore when Stamp asked her to accompany him to a film premiere, followed by supper at the Savoy. After showing reticence, Christie admitted that she did not have a suitable coat. Stamp gave her an open cheque and told her to find a winter coat. She turned up with a fur one, telling him that it cost £5 in the Portobello Road. 'At the reception, she nearly passed out with nerves,' recalled Stamp. 'Sarah Miles saw it coming and helped her into the powder room.'

The couple were often seen out dancing in the trendy Ad Lib disco, also frequented by David Bailey and Jean Shrimpton, and Roman Polanski and Sharon Tate, and Christie stayed at Stamp and Caine's flat for a while. 'It was like being with two blond gods of London,' she recalled. 'They were taller than anyone else, they were blonder than anyone else, they had such a lot of confidence, they just sort of

27

shone. The best thing about it was that they had a cleaner, and she made the most wonderful steak-and-kidney puddings.'

Stamp and Christie, whom he called 'Ruby Crystal', remained devoted to one another until she travelled north for location filming on *Billy Liar!*, the picture that was to launch her big-screen career, and wrote the actor a letter telling him that the romance was over.

Christie had by then already made her cinema debut, with director Ken Annakin casting her in two of his film comedies of the early 1960s, *Crooks Anonymous* and *The Fast Lady*. She acted in both alongside Stanley Baxter, Leslie Phillips and James Robertson Justice, all of whom had been in Annakin's previous screen comedy, *Very Important Person*.

Annakin was another who had seen Christie at the Central School of Speech and Drama. 'My daughter, Jane, who eventually became an agent, went to the school as well,' explained Annakin.

One day, she told me that she'd seen a performance by a girl there that she thought was terrific. I went to see Julie in a production at Central and liked her very, very much, so I invited her to our flat in Onslow Square, London. We talked, I decided then and there that she was very, very good, and put her in *Crooks Anonymous*.

She had no money at all. Money didn't seem to matter to her—she was very idealistic. So, because I had a car taking me to Beaconsfield Studios every day for filming, I used to pick her up from her flat in the Gloucester Road area and we would discuss the part in detail and what we would be doing that day. Basically, we ran a film school in the car for an hour every day. She was a wonderful student and listened very much.

When we were actually shooting, she was tremendously helpful and eager to do the right thing. She was very attentive to all the direction and was someone I felt would go a long way. Don't forget that at that time there were a lot of very good actors and actresses in England but I thought, with her attitude, paying a lot of attention to direction and being ambitious, she had a very good chance of getting on.

In *Crooks Anonymous*, Christie played a stripper who tries to persuade boyfriend Leslie Phillips to reform his villainous ways by enrolling with an organization called Crooks Anonymous. Although it was clear that Christie's good looks made her an ideal young female lead in the traditional style, Harry Fowler, who appeared in the picture as a former convict friend of Phillips, felt that she was entering pictures at a time when actresses were being given more scope:

Julie was excited about doing the film and aware of what it could lead to. She was very lucky because Ken was a comparatively modern director within the constrictions of making English films. It was the 1960s, which was the beginning of the change in social attitudes in this country. Young people began to be listened to, rather than frowned on. You had productions like *Saturday Night and Sunday Morning*, which opened the doors for British films to be more realistic, instead of stage plays put on to celluloid.

Previously, all the women in our films talked middle-class, even when they were acting cockneys, but that was the way it had been in the theatre. On screen, women were caricatured, like Diana Dors, who I'm sure wanted to play Lana Turner parts but had to settle for picture-postcard stereotypes.

In the 1960s, for the first time, you could actually have sex in films, and Julie oozed it. She was the first actress, apart from Shirley Anne Field, to have some semblance of real sex appeal. She was non-theatrical, both on and off screen. She also oozed confidence, but later told me that it wasn't an easy task as a beginner suddenly to be thrown among a band of very accredited actors who all knew what they were doing. There she was on her own with all these stalwarts of British pictures. She was slightly overawed, but she weathered it well and enjoyed it, and she was charming to work with.

Pauline Jameson, who acted in *Crooks Anonymous*, confirmed, 'Of course she was nervous, but Ken Annakin was very helpful.' Joyce Blair had fond memories of playing Christie's best friend in *Crooks Anonymous* but later found that the newcomer had no inclination to keep up their acquaintance:

I remember her being quite nervous but laidback about being nervous, and very ambitious. She was terribly nice at the time and we had a good laugh. We went off to High Wycombe to film her screen wedding and it was absolutely freezing. She was in her wedding dress and I was in my pink taffeta bridesmaid's dress. Underneath, I wore long johns and boots because it was so cold. She would have had something warm under her dress, too.

She had such a beautiful face, but I remember her putting on false nails in make-up. She was one of the lucky ones who went on to bigger things, but I think it was all to do with her looks. I never thought she was outstanding as an actress. You could never compare her to Meryl Streep, for example, but the camera loved her. She had a great-shaped face, but a terrible speaking voice, for me.

Also, Julie wasn't the warmest of people. I've worked with others who keep in touch. Julie wasn't like that. I don't think she'd know me from a hole in the wall if she saw me. In fact, I was starring in a play at the King's Head, in Islington, in the early 1980s and someone told me Julie was in the bar. I said, 'She'll probably come through to see me,' but she didn't. Not being a social butterfly doesn't make her a bad person, though.

After making *Crooks Anonymous* in black-and-white, many of the same actors and crew shot *The Fast Lady* in colour. Christie made an impression on one of those, actress Ann Beach, as 'a very lively, quite sexual and sensuous girl'. *The Fast Lady* featured Stanley Baxter as a gauche but obstinate Scottish civil servant—complete with kilt—learning to drive a vintage Bentley sports car in an attempt to win round girlfriend Christie's gruff tycoon father, played by James Robertson Justice, the larger-than-life star of the *Doctor* film comedies. The picture's high points include Baxter taking his driving test and, finally, the car—*The Fast Lady* of the title—being used to chase bank robbers.

Director Annakin was known to some actors as 'Panicky' Annakin because of his reaction when all did not go well, but *The Fast Lady* moved at a brisk pace, thanks to his slick direction. However, after her second picture there was still no guarantee that Christie would make it big on screen. The American trade paper *Variety* declared that she 'looks cute, but lacks the experience to build up a frail role as the love interest'.

BBC motor-racing commentator Raymond Baxter, who appeared in a dream sequence as himself interviewing Stanley Baxter, recalled 'rudimentary' sets and a 'charming and very pretty' Julie Christie. 'It was all very relaxed, very good fun,' he said. But the fun could not disguise the fact that both of Christie's first two films simply cast her as an appendage to the male stars—not entirely in keeping with the politics that she would espouse in years to come—and she admitted, 'It was a start, but I wasn't happy doing that sort of stuff.'

Two decades later, celebrated showbusiness journalist Peter Noble was perplexed to receive a request from Christie to omit *Crooks Anonymous* and *The Fast Lady* from her entry in his annual *Screen International Film and TV Year Book*, which included lists of stars and their films. His widow, the prolific character actress Marianne Stone, who was in both pictures, recalled, 'She wrote to Peter and asked him to take out those films—she didn't want to be associated with them. He was furious. It was ridiculous, he said, you can't just ignore your past—it's part of your career.'

Ken Annakin was shocked at Christie's apparent attempt to disown the films:

> I've been a little sad that she very rarely mentions that she was ever in those pictures, and she's a little scathing about that time because she had ambitions to do much more new-wave-type films, dramatic pictures which had a meaning. In interviews, she always tended to forget or pass over very quickly her beginnings in those comedies. It's as though she tried to say she's a natural actress who just stepped in and never did those films. But she worked with very interesting people like Stanley Baxter and James Robertson Justice—first-rate theatre and film actors—and obviously learned quite a bit from watching them, and I think my direction helped a great deal so that, when she did go into more serious stuff, she had the groundwork.

Whatever Christie thought about *Crooks Anonymous* and *The Fast Lady*, the money that she made from them enabled her to take a holiday and help out hard-up friends, a measure of her concern for others. 'Most of my friends are poor, you see,' said Christie at the time. 'I don't move around with a chi-chi crowd or anything and when I've got a bit of cash I'm inclined to share it around.'

Annakin recalled, 'When she got the money for her first film, she spent it immediately on a painting to help a young artist boyfriend out. That's the sort of person she was, very generous but not very practical. Julie was living a bohemian life. She had a big, straw bag filled with everything she needed if it turned out that she didn't want to go home. That was the time, the beginning of all young kids' strike for freedom.'

This generosity and free-living style perhaps reflected the socialist views that she had developed, in contrast to her conservative upbringing. The money was soon spent, but film fame and riches were not far away, although Christie had to suffer several rebuffs first.

Producers Harry Saltzman and Albert Broccoli, planning the first James Bond film, *Dr. No*, had already auditioned the young actress and turned her down. 'She was an absolute knockout,' said director Terence Young. 'I was mad about her . . . But Broccoli had reservations about her. He told Saltzman, "She's great, but she's no good for us. No tits." The role of white-bikinied Honey Ryder went to Swiss-born Ursula Andress, who had the required assets, and her international career as a screen glamour girl was launched.

Another director who believed in Christie was Michael Winner, who screen-tested her with two other actresses for *West 11*, one of his

35

early pictures, but the film's producer disagreed and overruled him. 'I thought she combined the talents of a wonderful actress with the attributes of a potential world star,' said Winner. However, the producer regarded her as no more than 'a B-film actress', so she did not get the part that eventually went to Kathleen Breck. But Christie was soon to prove Winner's eye for talent to be right.

However, she was not impressed when British-born Hollywood legend Cary Grant showed interest in her. The actor phoned British newspaper journalist Roderick Mann, who recalled, 'He'd seen a picture of her and he wanted to get in touch with her as he was casting a picture. Would I get her to ring him at his hotel? I rang Julie Christie and passed on the message. "What?" she said. "Cary Grant!" It went down with a dull thud . . . "OK," she said. "Thanks." She never did ring him.'

Christie's beauty and presence were also noticed on the social scene. Actor Tom Watson spotted her in the Salisbury public house, in St Martin's Lane, a short distance from London's West End theatres. At that time, it was frequented by actors, known and unknown. 'I remember her very clearly,' recalled Watson. 'The pub was crowded, I was speaking to James Villiers at the bar, and Peter O'Toole was there standing in the corner.

'Julie came in and sat at the bottom of the stairs leading to the first-floor rooms. There was a meeting of the Stage Golf Society upstairs and people were having problems getting past her. She looked very lovely, but very scatty—that look of ease about living and of having fun that people had in the 1960s, when they were free and easy. She was very alive, very vital.'

CHAPTER THREE

GIRL OF THE SWINGING SIXTIES

Christie's vitality was to turn her into a film star with the swing of a large handbag as she was seen walking down a street in the North of England in *Billy Liar!*, the acclaimed screen version of Keith Waterhouse and Willis Hall's stage play, based on Waterhouse's novel. As Billy's girlfriend, Liz, she represented not only his escape route but a symbol of the decade of liberation that was just under way as the music of the Beatles followed the socio-realistic books, plays and films that depicted the way life was lived by many people. 'When I saw that scene,' recalled Jeremy Kemp, a fellow-student at drama school, 'I thought, that's just an extension of her at Central. She was cheerful and upbeat—not at all reclusive and private in those days.'

The year of *Billy Liar!*'s release in the cinema, *1963*, signalled the real start of the Swinging Sixties, when pillars of the Establishment fell and young people's voices began to be heard. It was the year of the Profumo Affair, when government minister John Profumo was forced from office over his relationship with call-girl Christine Keeler, who had also been seeing a Russian diplomat, the year of President Kennedy's assassination and the year of the Beatles' first three number one singles.

Those who had grown up in Britain after the Second World War were putting the dull conservatism of the past behind them and challenging authority. The British pop music of the 1960s that followed the American rock 'n' roll invasion of the 1950s gave the chance of stardom to any group playing in pubs and clubs up and down the country, while cinemas were showing films that finally reflected working-class culture.

This was the era in which Christie was living and she wanted to act in films that portrayed it. Before making *Crooks Anonymous* and *The Fast Lady*, she had signed a three-picture deal with producers Independent Artists. Fortunately, after making it clear that she did not intend to fulfil the contract, the third picture fell through anyway and she was released. The promise she had displayed was to be given a stunning showcase by producer Joseph Janni and director John Schlesinger, who had watched Christie in *The Diary of Anne Frank* at the Central School of Speech and Drama, but had not seen her first two films.

There were plans for Lindsay Anderson, who directed *Billy Liar!* on stage, to make the screen version, but the rights eventually went to Janni, who with Schlesinger had already made *A Kind of Loving*, which was in the same vein. In early 1962, the pair were planning *Billy Liar!* and spotted Christie on the cover of a magazine, photographed with actor Cy Grant, both handcuffed and walking to St Martin-in-the-Fields Church, Trafalgar Square, on Human Rights Day to represent those around the world who were imprisoned for their beliefs. However, Janni and Schlesinger did not recognize her as the aspiring actress they had seen in the drama school production. At the same time, they were discussing the type of actress they wanted to play Liz—'a sort of earthy mother figure, a heavily breasted, all-enveloping creature,' said Schlesinger. 'There was a picture of this girl on the cover and a series of photographs inside. Very good pictures. Rather provocative. She looked scrumptious, absolutely marvellous. I didn't connect the girl in the picture with Julie.'

The producer and director invited Christie and two other actresses to screen tests on Hampstead Heath and at Waterloo Station with rising star Tom Courtenay, the Northern actor who had previously taken over Albert Finney's role as daydreamer Billy, living in his own, Walter Mitty world, in the West End stage play, and had made a stunning impression in his film debut, playing the rebel in director Tony Richardson's *The Loneliness of the Long Distance Runner.*

Christie did three screen tests in all, but she was not happy with them. Schlesinger said that, although the actress looked good, 'she came across terribly cold', and he regarded her as too 'chic' to play a girl from the provinces. The director subsequently watched her filming *Crooks Anonymous* at Beaconsfield Studios and was confirmed in his opinion after seeing that she had 'inches of make-up on and an unattractive hairstyle', so he and Janni opted for a soon-to-be-forgotten actress called Topsy Jane, who had previously starred with Courtenay in *The Loneliness of the Long Distance Runner.*

However, several weeks after filming started around Bradford and Leeds, she fell ill, so Janni and Schlesinger had to recast the part and reshoot Liz's scenes. They desperately viewed the screen tests again and concluded that Christie would fit the role. 'Jo and I knew Julie was pretty dreadful in *Crooks Anonymous*, which was being shown at the New Victoria [cinema] that week,' said Schlesinger, 'and we agreed that it would be better if we didn't go to see her in it. We met in the foyer of the cinema.'

As a result, Christie took over the part of Liz and, although nervous, was thrown into it with the long, memorable scene in which she is seen walking briskly along a Bradford street with the camera capturing every bit of her sparkling vitality as she swings her handbag, dodges traffic while crossing the road and pauses to look at a reflection of herself in a shop window. She appeared in the film for about ten minutes, but *Billy Liar!* proved to be her big break.

Rodney Bewes, who acted Billy's friend Arthur Crabtree, before finding his greatest fame on television in the situation comedy *The Likely Lads*, recalled the events leading to the switch of actresses, including Schlesinger's concern at her performance as witnessed in the daily 'rushes' of film shot. 'Topsy did a few weeks' filming and it became obvious from the "rushes" that nothing was coming across,' he explained. 'John asked me to take her to the cinema in the afternoons to get her out of herself. We used to sit in the front row, watching what ever was on, but it wasn't helping. It became clear that she was very ill, so Julie got the part. Because of the lateness of the hour, John gave her that tremendous introduction into the film, swinging her handbag along the street.' In fact, not all of that scene was filmed in Bradford. After

41

shooting the 'walk' sequence in that West Yorkshire industrial town, Schlesinger was not entirely happy with the results, filmed it again in London and edited together footage from both locations.

One scene that Topsy Jane had acted in was not reshot. Keith Waterhouse recalled:

A centrepiece sequence of *Billy Liar!* is the march-past of Billy's imaginary Ambrosian army, many hundreds strong, when he takes the salute from the balcony of Leeds Town Hall, together with his Eva Peron-type companion Liz. This scene, which took days to complete and required the services of legions of police to block off roads, was simply too expensive to reshoot. The close-up balcony shots were eliminated, but the long shots had to remain. Anyone who watches a video of *Billy Liar!* on television, and freezes the frame at the point where Billy and Liz are shown on the balcony, will see that Billy's consort is not Julie Christie at all but a mystery figure who appears nowhere else in the film—Topsy Jane.

The experience of working with Schlesinger was good for Christie. 'He was so gentle and courteous, and treated every single person with respect,' recalled Anna Wing, who acted Mrs Crabtree, Arthur's mother. 'If she was vulnerable and sensitive, she would respond to that instantly.'

At the beginning of her filming on *Billy Liar!*, Christie was still dating Terence Stamp and he watched her at work on a night shoot at King's Cross Station in freezing weather. She was so cold that he wrapped her in his sheepskin coat during gaps between takes. Then filming moved to the North of England and, while there, she ended the romance.

Although Christie's time on screen was short, Liz was central to the story. Billy Fisher is a daydreamer with a particularly vivid imagination who is sometimes unable to unravel truth from fiction. He escapes into a world of fantasy as an antidote to the drab normality of everyday life in a Northern town. In his job as an undertakers' clerk, he defrauds his bosses, Mr Shadrack and Mr Duxbury—memorably played by Leonard Rossiter and Finlay Currie—of stamp money. At home, he finds it difficult to communicate with his overbearing father and mild-mannered mother, acted by veterans Wilfred Pickles and Mona Washbourne.

On top of this, he is engaged to two young women, with an interchangeable ring being wrested from each 'to go back to the jeweller's for attention'. In Liz, the heroine of his fantasies, Billy finds someone who comes close to understanding him. She believes he has a real talent for writing and tries to persuade him that they could be happy together in

London, where he could try to find an outlet for his creativity. But, when she gets him as far as the railway station, his courage deserts him and he returns to the only reality he knows.

When the film was released in Britain, in the summer of 1963, acclaim for the production and its stars was immediate. There was even some recognition of Christie as a rising star in the United States, where the trade paper *Variety* remarked that 'Miss Christie turns in a glowing performance that will ultimately signpost a very successful career'. Thirty years later, the BBC and the British Film Institute jointly chose *Billy Liar!* among their 100 best films to celebrate the centenary of talkies.

Christie confessed that she had seen only a bleak future for herself before being screentested for *Billy Liar!* by Janni and Schlesinger. 'Before John Schlesinger asked me to do the test, I was really unhappy and struggling, an actress with no hope, just a sort of convent girl with blonde hair and a glimmer of a personality,' she said. 'John Schlesinger and Jo Janni changed all that and turned the tiny peep of light at the end of along tunnel of despair into a ray of hope for the future.'

The actress also later admitted to feeling satisfaction with the woman she portrayed in this early example of Britain's new-wave cinema, although she noted that men often retained their dominance in such pictures. 'In those films which we see as quite revolutionary—because it was the first time the working class was represented in film—women were not part of any revolution at all,' Christie told the feminist writer Beatrix Campbell. 'The boys were there to have women. A lot of them were about entrapment and hatred of women, and scoring. It was a boys' world. *Billy Liar!* was one of the best, because the girl chose not to go with Billy. She had her own life.' Christie reflected that she was probably 'the first woman who broke away from the Fifties model of the perfectly coiffed, perfectly presented woman', adding, 'Almost for the first time, there was a woman with stringy hair, who wore an old coat, and just pranced about and *was*.'

When filming ended on *Billy Liar!*, Christie took a holiday in Spain and returned briefly to television. She acted Betty Whitehead in a Granada Television production of J.B. Priestley's *Dangerous Corner*. Christie then played Roger Moore's niece in an episode of ITV's *The Saint*, the series based on the character of Simon Templar, the amateur sleuth created by novelist Leslie Charteris. It was ATV boss Lew Grade's first international hit, attracting viewers with its stories of Templar saving damsels in distress and solving crimes that baffled Chief Inspector Teal of Scotland Yard.

The Saint had begun in 1962 with the

debonair Moore taking the starring role that Patrick McGoohan had turned down; he felt that it was sexist, because Templar had an affair with a different woman every week. Other up-and-coming British actresses who had already appeared in the series included Suzan Farmer and Samantha Eggar, each with just a couple of films to their credit.

Christie played Templar's niece, Judith, of the episode's title. The story sees the sleuth trying to stop a fraud attempt, which switches from English country lanes to scenes of suspenseful adventure in the Swiss Alps—although the entire episode was in reality filmed in Britain, at Elstree Studios. In spite of being shot on film, unlike many television programmes that were still broadcast live, *The Saint* was originally made in black-and-white, but that did not prevent it from being screened in 106 countries.

During the episode, Christie and Moore shared a hotel bar scene. Ronald Wilson, who acted a desk clerk, was struck not just by this emerging actress's beauty, but also her stage fright. 'I remember her being strangely nervous for someone playing a leading part,' recalled Wilson, who shortly afterwards switched to directing television programmes. 'But Roger Moore was friendly, very understanding and helpful, going through the lines with her.'

Christie's career had taken off, but one

cloud on the horizon in 1963 was the death of her father, Frank, from a sudden heart attack, at the age of fifty-eight. Suffering from ill health, he had retired from tea planting in 1957 and planned to live out his years in Spain, where he bought a property in the Malaga region. However, he was too ill to go there, and instead stayed with his friends John and Doreen Haigh, in Beckenham, Kent. His illegitimate daughter, June, who had studied to university level in India, travelled to Britain with him and enjoyed a long career as a midwife, although she never married. In his will, Frank Christie left £5,000 to be invested for June and the rest of his British estate, valued at more than £19,000, to his estranged wife.

Three years earlier, Rosemary Christie had moved from the rural tranquillity of Gun Hill to the East Sussex town of Cuckfield. During that time, she had met someone who would bring out her academic side and be a partner until her death. Rosemary's interest in archaeology led her to take part in digs and, while on one, she met archaeologist Douglas Hague, who had a particular interest in castles and lighthouses. Having trained at Birmingham School of Art, he also produced many sketches and paintings.

This interest in art probably endeared him to Rosemary's daughter, as perhaps did his decision to accept agricultural work during the

47

Second World War as a conscientious objector. Hague was also concerned with conservation, and in the post-war years became an investigator with the Royal Commission on Ancient Monuments in Wales. He grew to love that country, and in 1964 Rosemary Christie bought a house in the Mid Wales village of Llanafan, about ten miles south-east of Aberystwyth, where they lived until her death eighteen years later. The couple appeared to be a good match. 'He thought she was a wonderful woman and she was very happy,' recalled Elsie White, Rosemary's former cleaner, who remained a lifelong friend. 'Douglas was a really interesting character. My husband and I used to have a lot of fun with him and Rosemary when we visited them in Wales.'

Julie Christie's own private life had moved into a happy phase after finding a boyfriend in 21-year-old Don Bessant, originally from Gillingham, Kent, who was studying at the Royal College of Art, in London. They had met just before Christmas 1962, when he was doing holiday work as a postman. Actor Freddie Jones, whose actress wife Jennifer Heslewood was in the same year as Christie at drama school and remained a lifelong friend, recalled Bessant as 'a charming young man, very handsome and quite big' after meeting him a few years later.

CHAPTER FOUR

DIFFERENT STAGES

By the time she was seen on television in *The Saint*, in October 1963, Christie had returned to the stage to get more experience. From June of that year, she spent six months with the prestigious Birmingham Repertory Company, which was celebrating its fiftieth anniversary. The company mixed modern works with the classics, and under its founder, Barry Jackson, had nurtured greats such as Albert Finney, Paul Scofield, Greer Garson and Laurence Olivier. Christie regarded repertory theatre as the backbone of drama. 'The fact that I've been successful in *Billy Liar!* hasn't changed my plans at all,' she said halfway through her run in Birmingham. 'Basic repertory training is an apprenticeship which any actor should serve—and, to be able to do this at Birmingham, one of the finest repertory companies in the world, is an even bigger advantage.'

Christie, who stayed in digs in the Moseley area of the city and was paid £16 a week by the theatre, enjoyed rehearsing one play during the day and performing another in the evenings, with a day off each week to return to London or visit her mother in Sussex.

The first of Christie's six plays with Birmingham Rep was a three-hour production of William Wycherley's Restoration comedy *The Country Wife*, in which she played Alithea. The bawdy play also saw the return to the theatre company of Sheila Gish (after changing her name from Gash), who later found some success in television and films. Throughout her run in Birmingham, Christie was overshadowed by another young actress, Linda Gardner, who played Mrs Margery Pinchwife in *The Country Wife*. 'Julie Christie, as her town-dweller sister, is pretty but has yet to gauge her voice-projection to the theatre,' the *Birmingham Evening Mail*'s critic wrote.

However, the actors' newspaper, *The Stage*, remarked on the 'sincerity and genuine fidelity in Julie Christie's endearing performance of Alithea', and Christie and the whole company had the bonus of performing the play at summer festivals in Antwerp and Zurich, which involved a 1,740-mile round coach trip.

She subsequently acted on the Birmingham stage in the Ben Travers farce *Thark*, Bertolt Brecht's *The Good Person of Szechwan*, Ronald Eyre's production of the James Saunders play *Next Time I'll Sing to You*, a translation of Jean Anouilh's seldom-performed *Colombe*, and a new revue, *Between These Four Walls*, which was written by Birmingham University dons Malcolm Bradbury and David Lodge and student Jim

Duckett.

The *Birmingham Evening Mail* critic failed to warm to Christie, though, noting that in *Next Time I'll Sing to You* she acted 'a lowbrow called Lizzie, who starts out with a Birmingham accent but tends to lose it during the evening'. After *Between These Four Walls*, he wrote of the production, 'It is amiable entertainment, sometimes nicely spiced, at others fatally corny (as in the BBC satire) and occasionally completely misguided (as when they ask the admirably decorative Julie Christie to sing a blues number).' This criticism of her vocals was echoed by the *Stratford-upon-Avon Herald*, whose critic contended that she 'must never again be allowed to sing unaccompanied'.

Otherwise, Christie's performances in Birmingham were mostly disregarded, even though *Billy Liar!* was released during her time there. She travelled to London for the British premiere and was allowed two days off to make an appearance at the Venice Film Festival in August, to promote the picture, while an understudy took her part in *The Good Person of Szechwan*. During rehearsals in Birmingham, Christie was noted for smoking and not wearing shoes. After performances, she boarded a bus to return to her digs.

As she approached the end of her time in Birmingham, Christie told Barry Norman, then writing for the *Daily Mail*, 'I've learned a lot. I think I'm a better actress now than when I got here. I think, too, that people here thought at first that they were going to be lumbered with some awful starlet. Perhaps they thought I'd be all upstage. Well, I was too terrified to upstage anyone. I had a terrible fear that I'd turn out to be the worst actress in the company. But I'm not. I think and hope that I've fitted in pretty well.'

Within a month of finishing at Birmingham Rep, Christie sought further stage experience by joining the Royal Shakespeare Company (RSC) to play Luciana in *The Comedy of Errors*. The production had first been performed by the company at its Stratford-upon-Avon home in 1962, before moving to the Aldwych Theatre, in London's West End, and being revived at Stratford the following year. In the original production, Luciana was played by director John Schlesinger's actress sister, Susan Marryott, who tragically died in 1963 after taking an overdose of sleeping tablets. This new production was part of a nine-week repertory season at the Aldwych, in January and February 1964, to mark the 400th anniversary of the Bard's birth.

The Stratford company, under directors Peter Hall, Peter Brook and Michel Saint-Denis, had adopted the name the Royal Shakespeare Company in 1961, a year after establishing a London base at the Aldwych. *The Comedy of Errors* joined *King Lear*, directed by Peter Brook and starring Paul Scofield, in repertory. Another newcomer to the RSC for this production was Michael Williams, early in an acclaimed career on stage and television. Also in the cast were Ian Richardson as Antipholus of Ephesus, Alec McCowen as Antipholus of Syracuse, Clifford Rose as Dromo of Ephesus, Diana Rigg as Luciana's older sister, Adriana, and Elizabeth Spriggs as A Courtezan.

The Aldwych staged eight performances, one of which included a moment of unplanned drama. Actor Wyn Jones collapsed on stage one night and was rushed to Charing Cross Hospital, where he was treated for an internal disorder, but the audience simply thought it was part of the show.

The 65-strong group of actors and RSC staff working on *King Lear* and *The Comedy of Errors* set off for a tour of Eastern Europe in the middle of February, sponsored by the British Council. While they travelled by air, five tons of settings and costumes was moved mostly by rail. Warsaw, Bucharest, Belgrade, Budapest, Prague, West Berlin, Helsinki, Leningrad and Moscow were all on the itinerary.

Audiences in the then Communist bloc were thrilled at the chance to see theatre performances of this calibre. Sold-out houses, standing ovations and critical acclaim in the press became a ritual. In Belgrade Yugoslavian

President Tito met the cast and crew after a performance of *King Lear*, and in Warsaw fans took to the stage a giant basket of pink carnations, which were rare and exotic flowers in a Polish winter.

In Moscow, a day before *The Comedy of Errors* opened, journalist John Gardner of the *Stratford-upon-Avon Herald* enjoyed time spent socializing with Christie and two other actresses. They went to see Struchkova dance *Giselle* at the Bolshoi, before watching the English Language Amateur Drama Group enthusiastically rehearsing *The Dream*. 'After the rehearsal, we are asked to criticize,' wrote Gardner in a diary-type account of his visit to Moscow. 'The girls show great tact. I am suitably restrained, though we do point out that love-in-idleness should be a blue flower and not a dirty great red tulip—which Oberon has been brandishing like a mace.' In Moscow Christie also enjoyed time off to see the works of art in the Kremlin, and in Leningrad visited the Hermitage.

When the East European tour came to an end, the whole RSC entourage left for North America, although that part of the tour was not sponsored by the British Council. The change in climate during that plane trip was dramatic, from a freezing, snow-covered Moscow to sunshine and the lush, green landscape of New England. The company performed in Washington, Boston and

Toronto, before finishing in New York. After seeing *King Lear* and *The Comedy of Errors* on Broadway, *Variety*'s critic, 'Hobe', asserted that the seriousness of the first was complemented well by the 'unashamed entertainment' of the second and described Christie as 'a decorative and spirited sister' to Diana Rigg's Adriana.

Roger Howells, a stage manager on both productions at the Aldwych and on tour, believed that acting in only one of the two plays might have been 'a bit isolating' for Christie. 'Perhaps she felt slightly outside the magic circle,' he said.

Many of the actors were in both *King Lear* and *The Comedy of Errors*. Consequently, she had a certain amount of time to herself on tour. Also, she hadn't worked with others in the company before. But her performance was wholly professional, although there was an element of insecurity there, perhaps because she had some responsibility in a semi-leading role and was aware that there was expectation of her through being a cinema star in the making. Also, she was enormously popular with the young men in the company and quite a few were very happy to hang around and escort her.

One of those 'young men' was Peter Tory, later to become a journalist and newspaper columnist.

When the long tour came to an end, the RSC group left New York on a charter British Airways flight, complete with sets and props. 'I remember sitting in the aircraft, waiting to take off,' recalled Clifford Rose, who acted in both *King Lear* and *The Comedy of Errors*. 'The captain was walking down the aisle, looking at all the scenery and then at the cast coming on board. We all had an enormous amount of luggage, including gifts we had picked up over the weeks. Then Julie got on, carrying a huge, heavy, cast-iron coffee mill and the captain said, "I think we should check the payload before we take off." He wasn't joking.'

On their return to Britain, Christie and the company staged a special production for the Queen and her guests at Windsor Castle during Ascot Week, in June. Early that morning, they left London on a coach, accompanied by journalists. The press waited outside the front gates of the castle while the company went inside, had lunch and rehearsed before their performance in the Waterloo Chamber that evening before the Queen, Duke of Edinburgh and Princess Margaret. 'It was the first time that a complete play had been performed at Windsor Castle since early Elizabethan times,' recalled Pauline Jameson, who played Aemilia and had previously acted in Christie's first film, *Crooks Anonymous*.

'The tour had been very special and it was an honour to appear at Windsor.'

The event gave Christie good training for a time later in her career when she would give few media interviews. 'After the Ascot people's dinner, the company joined the guests and the Royal Family for a party until about two in the morning,' explained Jameson. 'When we got back on the coach, we picked up the press and I felt so proud of all these actors, because the journalists clearly wanted to hear snippets of information about what the Queen or Prince Philip had said, but nobody said anything.'

Although the experience of theatre was useful, the highly strung Christie—who admitted to smoking, chewing her fingernails and biting her cuticles—vowed thereafter to concentrate on screen roles. While in the United States, MGM had negotiated with her London agent for her to play a whore called Daisy Battles in *Young Cassidy*, a film about the life of the great Irish dramatist Sean O'Casey. He died that year and was noted for plays such as *Juno and the Paycock* and *The Plough and the Stars*, which depicted working-class life in his native Dublin and the struggle for Irish independence.

Based on O'Casey's autobiography, *Mirror in My House*, John Whiting's script featured John Cassidy as the playwright's screen persona. Opening in 1911, the film traces his involvement in the events surrounding Irish opposition to British rule, a period that shaped O'Casey's political thinking and writing, as well as his personal life.

Young Cassidy was to be made in Dublin by veteran director John Ford, an Irish-American whose 200 films included such classics as *How Green Was My Valley* and John Wayne Westerns. Ford had a real feel for characters and was also notable for making pictures that captured the atmosphere of the great outdoors.

Filmed in a slum area in the north of Dublin near Mountjoy Square, close to O'Casey's childhood home, *Young Cassidy* successfully depicted the poverty of the city in the early years of the twentieth century. However, Ford had to leave the production through illness just a couple of weeks into the shooting schedule. He was replaced by Jack Cardiff, a British cinematographer noted for his inventive camerawork in pictures such as *Black Narcissus. His* earlier experience working on travelogues helped him to establish a unique style and a sympathy for the feel that Ford was trying to evoke in *Young Cassidy.*

The film starred Rod Taylor in the lead role of John Cassidy and, as well as Christie, introduced other relative film newcomers Maggie Smith and Siân Phillips. In her main contribution to the picture, Christie's barmaid wastes no time in jumping into bed with Rod Taylor's hero—a scene edited for American release—while outside a bloody riot continues. After the love-making is over, Daisy smiles contentedly and tells John how fabulous he is. Her smile remains in glorious close-up as her hero walks out of the door. Again, with little screen time, Christie lent her own special sparkle to a film.

Everything directed by Ford, including that love scene, was incorporated in the first twenty minutes of the picture, but the spectacular riot sequence—set during a tram drivers' strike—was one mistakenly credited to him by many critics who compared his direction with that of Cardiff. 'I suppose I should have been flattered that my work should be considered to be the work of the master,' recalled Cardiff, 'but in fact I was indignant. I measured John Ford's work on the film. It totalled four and a half minutes out of two hours' screen time. I wrote blistering letters to the critics, but it never does any good.'

Christie herself received little attention from critics when the film was released in Britain and the United States at the start of 1965, with most of the acting plaudits going to Taylor and Smith. 'But there were many other, well known actors in *Young Cassidy* who were hardly noticed,' recalled Pauline Delany, who played Cassidy's girlfriend Bassie Ballynoy. 'Michael Redgrave, Edith Evans and Flora Robson were all there. I never met Julie Christie while filming, but I think she had an operation during the making of it.' In fact, she had been taken ill on the flight to Dublin and rushed to hospital, where she was diagnosed with peritonitis.

However low-profile Christie was in *Young Cassidy*, others in the business were keen to work with her after the impact she had made on screen in *Billy Liar!* Charlton Heston wanted Christie to star with him in the medieval melodrama *The War Lord*, a Hollywood screen adaptation of Leslie Stevens's stage play *The Lovers*. He even organized a private screening of *Billy Liar!* for Universal Studios executives, but they refused to pay her the fee demanded. 'I tried very hard to get her,' explained Heston, 'and I could have, for $35,000, which her agents were asking. Universal balked at the fee and wanted someone cheaper. It would have been a bargain. She was on the brink of becoming an international star.' Instead Canadian newcomer Rosemary Forsyth took the part of Bronwyn, but that actress's early promise foundered. Much of her subsequent career was spent in American TV movies.

Christie proved to be very discerning about the roles she accepted. Back in 1962, at the time she was filming *Billy Liar!*, she had signed a four-year contract with producer Joseph Janni. This effectively made her his property to use in a guaranteed number of his own films with director John Schlesinger, or to hire out to other producers and directors. Janni paid her an annual salary, whether she worked or not, and she received 50 per cent of the money paid to her, minus that salary, for films she made with others. Within a few years, the salary increased to reflect her growing bankability—she went from being paid £8,000 per film to more than £150,000, and the contract was extended until 1968. By then, she had become an international star.

CHAPTER FIVE

CINEMA'S NEWEST DARLING

It was *Darling*, produced and directed by the team of Joseph Janni and John Schlesinger, that made Christie a worldwide star and won her the Best Actress Oscar for her vivacious performance as the immoral and irresponsible young model who leaves her husband for a television journalist, before hopping into bed with other men.

Clearly intended to be a 'fashionable' film, Schlesinger drew on his background in television documentaries to make the black-and-white picture in a 'realistic' style intended to reflect the new freedoms enjoyed—and sometimes abused—in the Swinging Sixties. The bittersweet film also showed the exploitation of a woman who enjoys sexual adventures and defies convention but pays for this with unhappiness. Each apparent high point is followed by some form of punishment.

This shallowness was reinforced with a restrained musical soundtrack by bandleader John Dankworth, who had previously written the score for director Tony Richardson's landmark film *Saturday Night and Sunday Morning.* 'The theme is the destruction of the female principle, the turning of a person into a commodity,' said Frederic Raphael, who wrote the original screenplay.

Christie played Diana Scott—called 'Darling' by all—a model whose career progresses to cover girl and and film starlet. Invited to tell her story in *Ideal Woman* magazine, Diana's words from the interview are heard over the pictures as a commentary on her life. She cheats on her husband after meeting the more sophisticated television interviewer and would-be novelist Robert Gold, acted by Dirk Bogarde, who leaves his wife and children to set up home with her. But she does the same to him when she has an affair with influential public relations executive Miles Brand, played by Laurence Harvey, who had so memorably acted Joe Lampton in *Room at the Top.* After Robert leaves Diana, she accepts a marriage proposal from an Italian prince, played by Jose Villalonga.

Humour and irony also play a part in *Darling*. In one scene, Diana and Robert, then still married to others, return from Southampton and phone their respective spouses to say that they have been delayed. Each acts as telephone operator for the other, creating the impression that they are speaking long-distance. Diana later tries the same trick on Robert after a trip to Paris with Miles.

Other significant events in the film include Diana going on a shoplifting expedition at the London department store Fortnum and Mason's and having an abortion after discovering that she is expecting Robert's baby. As a result of the operation, Diana declares that she wants no more to do with sex and, giving an insight into her nymphomania, adds that she never enjoyed it anyway.

When *Darling* received its world premiere as the official British entry at the Moscow Film Festival, in the Kremlin Palace of Congress in July 1965, some sequences were cut, including one in which Christie strips off before leaving her Italian prince. However, the picture was seen in its entirety throughout the Western world.

In Britain, the *Observer* commented that the film was 'strong stuff' with 'transvestite scenes, corruption and lovemaking of a frankness hardly conceivable in a British film'. In one ground-breaking scene, Laurence Harvey performs simulated cunnilingus on Christie.

This was a subject that had previously hardly been touched on in the cinema, although American director Joseph H. Lewis caused controversy with his 1955 crime thriller *The Big Combo*, in one of whose love scenes actor Richard Conte's head is seen making its way down a young woman's body and disappearing out of the bottom of the picture. Summoned to the Breen Office, the American equivalent of the then British Board of Film Censors, Lewis was asked to explain where Conte is actually supposed to be going. He replied innocently, 'How the hell do I know where he went? Maybe he went for a cup of coffee.' After more debate, the sequence was left in the film, although directors were not quick to follow with scenes of this simulated—in fact, unseen—act, until the success of *Darling* established that this previously taboo subject could be tackled. After Harvey's head disappears out of the bottom of the picture, too, Christie's face responds, although Raphael's script for this scene noted that Miles and Diana 'seduce each other very coolly, in ritual, never as part of a relationship, never in mutual joy'. Several decades later, this and the other then daring scenes featured in *Darling* seem very tame, but at the time such a film was considered courageous for portraying a woman on screen in this way.

The picture's ultimate accolade came when Christie won the Oscar for Best Actress.

Ironically, *Darling* was a production that came to the screen only after a long fight by Janni and Schlesinger to get financial backing and keep Christie in the starring role. The pair had started discussing the project while making *Billy Liar!* in 1962. Radio disc jockey Godfrey Winn, who made a cameo appearance in that film, told them the true story of a model who became the shared mistress of a group of men. They provided her with a flat, making her accessible to all of them, but she eventually committed suicide.

Janni paid Winn to write a ten-page synopsis of the story and discussed with John Schlesinger and Frederic Raphael the possibility of turning it into a film. 'We started with the idea of the ghastliness of the present-day attitude of people who want something for nothing,' explained Schlesinger. 'Diana Scott, the principal character, emerged in the script of *Darling* as an amalgam of various people we had known.' Schlesinger and Janni's further research included an interview with a young career woman about her public and private life.

However, once the shooting script was finished, it was turned down by a string of major distribution companies and potential backers, including Columbia, which found the story unsavoury, and Britain's National Film Finance Corporation, which considered the heroine too unsympathetic. Others were unwilling to part with the £400,000 needed to make *Darling* because Christie was a relative unknown. Janni was told that using an actress such as Shirley MacLaine would guarantee him the money, but he was determined to stick with the actress who had shown so much promise in *Billy Liar!*

When Christie was touring North America with the Royal Shakespeare Company, he flew there to see her and, at the same time, search for a Hollywood star to play Robert. The role was rejected by several top stars, and Montgomery Clift met Schlesinger to talk about it, but the actor had been involved in a serious car accident that left him with a scarred face and concussion. Drugs and alcohol had also taken their toll and Clift and the director agreed that he was not right for the part. In fact, the one-time romantic lead died a couple of years later, in 1966.

The search went on to find an actor suitable to play the role. Schlesinger said:

It was originally written as an American journalist wandering about Europe. Nobody would touch it—Paul Newman, even Cliff Robertson turned it down. Nobody wanted to know. Julie was in Philadelphia appearing in *The Comedy of Errors.* I didn't go and see her. For one thing, I gathered she was not brilliant in it and, for another, she was playing the same part my sister had played at Stratford. And she had died recently. I couldn't face it. I spent three days working with Julie, just reading in my hotel room. I came back to London knowing I thought the areas which she would find difficult. I was right about one of them, wrong about the other. I thought she would have difficulty in maturing into the middle-class rich woman. She brought it off perfectly. But she found it hard to deal with the hipper, more camp elements which are not part of her personality. Nevertheless, I knew she could play it.

Holding out to keep Christie as the star, Janni eventually found backing in Britain from Anglo Amalgamated, as well as ploughing almost all of his own money into the production, mortgaging his car and flat to do so. Schlesinger also found a leading actor in Dirk Bogarde. He took him to lunch and admitted that Gregory Peck and others had turned down the part and that the casting of Christie had led to difficulties in getting finance. Bogarde told Schlesinger, 'I want to work with you and I want to work with Christie,' adding that he had previously seen her on television in *A for Andromeda* and considered her to represent 'the young', with whom he wanted to act.

However, Schlesinger was not entirely convinced that Bogarde—a big star in 1940s and 1950s films such as *The Blue Lamp*, *A Tale of Two Cities* and the *Doctor* series—was right for the role, fearing that he was too '*soigné*' and not like the intellectual television interviewer in baggy flannels that he was to play. But the actor was confirmed in the role after a 'style test' meeting was arranged to which he turned up in his old gardening clothes and a knitted tie. In fact, *Darling* was one of the first films—along with, most notably, *The Servant*—to help Bogarde shed the matinée-idol mantle that he so resented.

All those involved in *Darling* gave it their utmost. During three-and-a-half months' filming, mostly in Britain, but with a few scenes shot in Italy and Capri, Christie had only two days off. 'I have never worked so hard in my life,' she said. 'It was awful—we just didn't even stop on Sundays. I was exhausted at the end of it.'

Throughout the shoot, Anglo Amalgamated kept a close eye on the production. At the end of the first week, one of the company's representatives weighed in with his thoughts about Christie, exclaiming to Bogarde's friend and agent Tony Forwood, 'She's got a face like the back of a bus. She looks just like a feller! Look at that jaw . . . she could play bloody football. Don't you agree? She's dead ugly.' To this, Forwood replied, 'I think she's the nearest thing I've seen to Brigitte Bardot.'

The film proceeded, shot mostly at

Shepperton Studios, but the budgetary problems resurfaced when, halfway through, Janni asked Bogarde to accept a cut in his salary and 'defer your deferments'. Like Bogarde, Christie received a salary and was guaranteed a share of the film's profits—if it made any.

However, the money problems did not stop Forwood from helping out Christie when she needed a new bed. By then, she shared a noisy flat in Earl's Court, west London, with Don Bessant and some stray cats that she had rescued. She slept on an airbed, echoing her first days at drama school, but one night it sprang a leak. The next morning, while filming at Paddington Station, Christie apologized if she looked tired, said she was saving for a brass bed that she had seen in a King's Road junk shop and asked a member of the crew to get some puncture patches from a nearby garage. Forwood wrote out a cheque to enable her to buy the bedstead and Bogarde wrote another to pay for a mattress. 'Ta,' she said, with a beaming smile. Bogarde, already a veteran of more than forty films, found the experience of working with Christie a delight and credited her with teaching him more about ad-libbing than anyone else.

Despite reservations by some critics, who believed the characters to be cold and the picture's moral stance confused, *Darling* was widely recognized as a significant film. The issues of morality and the way women were portrayed on screen were being debated in a way that would have been inconceivable five years earlier, at the start of the decade.

The celebrated critic Kenneth Tynan remarked in the *Observer* that Diana was 'a composite figure whose component parts do not entirely fit' and Penelope Houston wrote in *Sight and Sound* that the character was 'stripped for stripping's sake'. The film's advertising campaign featured a photograph of Christie as Diana, apparently naked, lying on a bed, with inset pictures of Bogarde and Harvey either side. This represented Diana as the object of male desire, but her smile also symbolized the sexual freedom and pleasure that a woman could experience, although Christie herself later voiced reservations about removing her clothes on screen.

She had not wanted to do the scene in *Darling* in which Diana strips in front of a mirror, but Schlesinger insisted, cleared the set of unnecessary technicians and filmed it in one take. 'I hate undressing,' said Christie almost two years after the film's release. 'As when they forced me to do it in those scenes in *Darling*, just like that, in front of everybody. I was so ashamed. Those damned electricians watching me, and the cameraman and the whole damned cast. I'm not the type of woman to undress so light-heartedly. I'm too modest.'

More than twenty years later, when her own

ideas on feminism and the portrayal of women on screen were more developed, Christie would also question the way she played the role. 'That was supposed to be about a woman who did her own thing,' she said. 'But it wasn't—it was about a woman who did her own thing and was punished . . . I quite enjoyed playing a very, very selfish woman. If I played her now, with what I now know, I'd try to portray that selfishness as worthwhile instead of naughty and doomed.'

But, at the time, the film made waves. Christie won a New York Film Critics Award for Best Actress and the same writers named *Darling* the best English-language picture of 1965 and John Schlesinger best director. The greatest honours came at the Oscars ceremony, with Christie nominated as Best Actress, facing competition from Julie Andrews for *The Sound of Music*, Samantha Eggar for *The Collector*, Simone Signoret for *Ship of Fools* and Elizabeth Hartman, the only American nominee, for *A Patch of Blue*. Christie travelled to the United States for the ceremony, at the Santa Monica Civic Auditorium, on 18 April 1966, and on hearing that she had won the Best Actress honour faced up to her fear of going on stage to accept the small, gold-plated Academy Award statuette.

Two decades later, Christie explained to television interviewer Michael Aspel how daunting this was. 'One of the things that's left over from school is an absolute terror of hearing my name pronounced in public,' she told him. 'In fact, when you introduced me, I thought, "Oh, my God, I'm going to be brought up in front of the assembly for some heinous crime and be humiliated." And that was, I think, the feeling when I got the Oscar—"I've got to go up there. What am I going to do?" I think I burst into tears, to my shame.'

Darling also won Oscars for screenplay writer Frederic Raphael and costume designer Julie Harris. Before collecting her honour, Christie had already caused ructions at the ceremony when, about to present another award, she stepped on to the stage wearing a polka-dot chiffon mini-dress. It was an indication that, with the world at her feet, she would not conform to the rules.

CHAPTER SIX

JOINING THE REVOLUTION

Even as *Darling* was being filmed, news began to filter out about this new star who was about to take the cinema world by storm. Celebrated British director David Lean, best known for pictures such as *Brief Encounter, Bridge on the*

River Kwai and *Lawrence of Arabia*, as well as definitive screen versions of Charles Dickens's *Great Expectations* and *Oliver Twist*, was casting for his film version of *Doctor Zhivago*, based on Boris Pasternak's novel about the Russian Revolution, and asked to see film of both Christie and Bogarde's work.

Christie had been brought to the attention of Lean by his production designer, John Box, who won an Oscar for his work on the director's previous epic, *Lawrence of Arabia*. 'I saw *Billy Liar!* and was very impressed with the film and this young lady whom I hadn't seen before,' recalled Box. 'I told David, "I'm not going to tell you why, but there's a film you must see." We actually watched it in Stockholm while on a recce for *Zhivago*. At the end of the screening, David said, "You're absolutely right, John." But I wasn't! I had foreseen Julie playing the part of Zhivago's wife, whereas he said, "That was Lara—we need look no further." '

Lean asked John Schlesinger to send him 'rushes' of Christie in *Darling*. Meanwhile, Bogarde asked permission from American director Joseph Losey to send a reel of *King and Country*, one of his two most recent films. Bogarde heard no more, but Christie learned that she had landed the part of Zhivago's free-spirited mistress, Lara, as the pair filmed on the lawns of Skindles, in Maidenhead, Berkshire. She was sitting on the grass in a tweed suit and pearls, dressed for the scene they were shooting, and reading Karl Marx in paperback, when she was summoned to the telephone. Returning quietly, Christie was asked by Bogarde what the news was. 'I've got Lara,' she replied. 'Rather good. But they want me to get out of this little picture . . . said it wasn't important and that I should get to Madrid as soon as possible and start working on the part. They say I could get an Oscar for it, that I should leave John and all this . . .'

Asked what she would do, Christie's eyes were, according to Bogarde, filled with tears of outrage. She said, 'I told them to stuff Lara or wait. They'll bloody have to wait. Leave this? Leave John, all this? What kind of business is this?' In the event, Lean waited and Joseph Janni was able to get extra finance to finish *Darling* by selling Christie's services to him under the contract they had signed after making *Billy Liar!*

Christie flew to Madrid for a screen test, content if she ended up with only a free holiday—until she met the director. 'He bowled me over with his force,' recalled Christie. 'He made me feel he wanted something and I would give it to him.' Lean was certain that he had the right actress for the role of a character who had to age from seventeen to forty on screen and described in Pasternak's novel as 'unequalled in spiritual beauty—martyred, stubborn, extravagant, crazy, irresponsible, adored'.

So Christie found herself again acting alongside *Billy Liar!* star Tom Courtenay, who now played Pasha, a student revolutionary. The politicized nurse Lara marries him before he leaves her and turns into a heartless Red general known as Strelnikov. Featured as Yuri Zhivago, who subsequently becomes Lara's passionate lover, was Omar Sharif, with Geraldine Chaplin as his childhood sweetheart Tonya. Other leading roles were taken by Rod Steiger, Alec Guinness, Ralph Richardson, Siobhan McKenna and Rita Tushingham.

Although widely panned by critics, the film eventually became Lean's biggest box-office success. It was another of his sweeping epics, even surpassing *Lawrence of Arabia* in some of its visuals, with outstanding cinematography by veteran Freddie Young and spectacular production design by John Box. As always, the director—who had learned his craft by editing newsreels in the 1930s—planned *Doctor Zhivago* meticulously and executed each scene with precision.

But the picture came to the screen only after a difficult history of gaining rights and getting a suitable cast together. Pasternak's novel about a humble poet-doctor caught up in the events of the Russian Revolution, written in a poetic style that some now regard as pretentious, had been banned in the Soviet Union because of its unflattering accounts of the way in which the Bolsheviks seized power in 1917 and the subsequent hardships under the Communist regime. But copies of the book were smuggled out of the country, and in 1958, at the height of the Cold War between East and West, Pasternak was awarded the Nobel Prize for Literature, although the Soviet government persuaded him not to accept it.

Many film studios and executives sought the rights to *Doctor Zhivago* before Italian producer Carlo Ponti signed a deal with the book's publisher in that country, Feltrinelli, in late 1962. Ponti then entered into negotiations with MGM president Robert O'Brien. They agreed that the personal story told against a background of fateful historical events would be best translated to the big screen by David Lean, who had just made *Lawrence of Arabia*, winner of seven Oscars. As a result, Lean read the story while sailing from Britain to the United States, and by the time he reached New York was intent on making the film.

He decided that Robert Bolt, who had scripted *Lawrence of Arabia*, was one of the few dramatists capable of writing the screenplay of *Doctor Zhivago*. Lean was adamant that characters would not be tailored to fit specific stars, but actors and actresses would be chosen according to the roles. Bolt, who calculated that the complete novel would take forty-five hours to film, then spent a year working on a lengthy 'treatment', on which his

284-page screenplay was based.

Casting then proved a major hurdle. Lean wanted Alec Guinness to play Zhivago's brother, Yevgrav. Guinness, a veteran of four of the director's previous films, from *Great Expectations* and *Oliver Twist* to *The Bridge on the River Kwai* and *Lawrence of Arabia*, presented no problems, but he had to fight for Christie.

Producer Ponti was married to actress Sophia Loren, one of the cinema world's leading ladies, and Lean feared that he would push for her to take the role of Lara. Although he did not actually ask Lean to consider her, Ponti invited the director and Barbara Cole, his continuity girl and lover, to a dinner at which Loren arrived, according to Cole, 'in a little plain dress with a lace collar, looking very innocent, speaking very good English and being really very nice'. On returning home, Lean told Cole, 'If anyone can convince me she's a virgin, I'll let her play the part.'

Lean subsequently wrote to Robert O'Brien of MGM explaining why he needed a young actress in the role, centring his argument on a scene in which Komarovsky, played by Rod Steiger, seduces Lara. 'Most actresses will be able to cope with the introductory scenes,' wrote Lean. 'The real test begins from the moment Komarovsky starts his seduction. The key to this scene is the girl's genuine aura of youthful innocence. She must be caught in an experience quite new to her . . . This is why I want a young actress. Innocence cannot be acted except on a superficial level. I would not believe this was Miss Loren's first encounter with sex and, if I don't believe it, I would think she's a bitch.'

After Loren was effectively removed from the running, Robert Weitman of MGM suggested Yvette Mimieux for the role. Lean himself asked Bolt what he thought about Sarah Miles, to which the writer replied, 'No, no, no, she's just a North-country slut.' Ironically, Bolt later married Miles—twice. Jane Fonda was also mentioned for the part, with the possibility of dubbing her voice to avoid criticism of the actress's American accent. Lean also mentioned French actress Jeanne Moreau, but Bolt was vehemently opposed to this idea.

Then John Box suggested that Lean watch *Billy Liar!*, and the director was bowled over by Christie's screen presence. Concerned about casting a relative newcomer in such an important role, he phoned John Ford, who had directed her in *Young Cassidy* before illness forced him to hand over to Jack Cardiff. 'She's great, the best young actress that has ever come into the business,' Ford told Lean. 'No one in the past has shown so much talent at such an early age.'

Finding an actor to play the central role of Yuri Zhivago had been no easier. MGM wanted Paul Newman but Lean, who went to see him in *The Prize*, his latest picture for the studio, had grave doubts about the actor playing a dreamer. MGM president O'Brien was opposed to Lean's idea of using Max von Sydow, and Bolt could not bear producer Ponti's suggestion of Burt Lancaster.

Lean believed that his *Lawrence of Arabia* star, Peter O'Toole, would be right for the part. However, on seeing an early version of the script, O'Toole pronounced it terrible. In any case, producer Sam Spiegel refused to release O'Toole from his commitment to the Second World War drama *The Night of the Generals.* Eventually, Barbara Cole came up with the idea of approaching Omar Sharif, who accepted. Any criticism of an Egyptian playing a Russian was forestalled by pulling Sharif's eyes back with tape and straightening his hair.

After Christie was cast, Lean considered her former lover, Terence Stamp, to take the dual role of Pasha/Strelmkov, but then settled on Tom Courtenay. The director initially approached Marlon Brando to play the lecherous Komarovsky, who seduces Lara, but received no reply to his letter. Lean then wanted James Mason, who was keen, but eventually cast Rod Steiger. Geraldine Chaplin, daughter of legendary film comedian Charlie, was chosen to play Zhivago's devoted wife, Tonya, who had been the hero's child sweetheart. Siobhan McKenna acted Tonya's mother and Ralph Richardson her father, and Rita Tushingham played Lara and Zhivago's grown-up lovechild.

The cast was brought together outside Madrid on 28 December 1964. 'David Lean said he wanted Julie to be received terribly well,' recalled Nicolas Roeg, who started work as director of photography on the picture before disagreements with the director led him to leave. 'He made sure there were flowers and champagne waiting when she arrived. She enjoyed that but was able to laugh at it as well—the idea of it tickled her.'

Spain was chosen for the picture's principal locations because of its snow-covered mountains that would serve as the Urals, vast plains resembling the steppes of Siberia and the only widetrack railway system in Europe outside Russia. Lean had been invited to go to that country but believed the authorities would simply try to talk him out of making the film, given that Pasternak's novel was still banned there. Lean decided to use Spain for most of the shoot after looking for locations in Canada, Yugoslavia and Scandinavia. The country was also attractive because the Spanish dictator, Franco, offered incentives that made it cheap to film there.

The production of *Doctor Zhivago* was mammoth, with the final budget spiralling to $15 million. To accommodate many of the huge sets, MGM leased the entire CEA Studios in the Canillas suburb of Madrid and built an additional sound stage there, the largest in Spain. An enormous exterior set was constructed on a ten-acre site near Madrid airport to represent the streets of central Moscow, including the Kremlin and other landmarks, and almost a mile of track was laid through these streets for the tram cars. To create the Urals scenes, Lean and production designer John Box settled on a location three hours north, on the Spanish plains near Soria. For the depiction of deep snows and wintry vistas in Siberia, Finland was used for the first time in a major film. The making of the picture was itself filmed, by director Thomas Craven, for a documentary feature entitled *Zhivago: Behind the Camera with David Lean.*

While shooting in Madrid, in temperatures of up to 120 degrees fahrenheit, Christie—like Steiger, Sharif and Chaplin—lived in an MGM-rented apartment in the city, comprising one bedroom, a living room and kitchen, while the rest of the cast and crew stayed in hotels. On set, Lean succeeded in getting Christie to leave behind her reputation for underplaying and to let herself go. 'I went over the top,' she said. 'It was exciting.' But Lean was not averse to shouting at the actress to get the best from her. Alec Guinness was witness to one of his reprimands. 'My most vivid recollection is of arriving on the set the

81

day I arrived in Madrid, to say hello to David Lean, to hear him bawling Julie out for slightly crumpling the dress she was wearing,' recalled Guinness. 'He reduced her to tears, which wasn't helpful to anyone.' Costume designer Phyllis Dalton observed:

It was quite a tough film, and working with David Lean was a seven-days-a-week job. Julie was very young, disciplined enough acting wise but not necessarily in herself. You could dress Geraldine Chaplin and she would stay absolutely immaculate 12 hours at a time, but Julie was untidy and needed more looking after. One had to tell the wardrobe staff to watch her. It was our job to keep her looking at least the same as she was in the previous shot! I doubt if Julie and David were very close. David was often closer to technicians than to actors. He was marvellous with his chosen team, who worked with him a lot, but he could be quite cruel to actors.

More trouble came when Christie was required to wear a bright-red dress designed by Phyllis Dalton for the scene in which Lara is seduced by Komarovsky. 'Julie wouldn't wear it because she hated red,' production designer John Box explained.

So Phyllis came to me and asked what I

could do to help, because David Lean held me responsible for the general look of the picture. I couldn't find Julie at first, but eventually I did so and asked her, 'What's the trouble about this dress, Julie? We don't want to go and talk to David about it.' She was upset and said, 'I hate red. I hate this dress.' I said, 'The whole point is that it's a dress bought for you by Komarovsky, who wants your body. Obviously, in the film you hate the dress. It's Komarovsky's dress, and the fact that you hate it yourself works beautifully.' She said, 'Right.' And she wore it.

Whatever her costume, Lean believed Christie's eyes were one of her greatest attributes and instructed director of photography Freddie Young to ensure that audiences saw them to their best effect. So a 'pup' light was put under the camera lens to illuminate them. Christie was happy to hand herself over to Lean as the director. 'My tendency was to put myself in the position of a child, and David was paternalistic,' she recalled. 'He behaved like an authoritarian but kindly father . . . After the rape scene, for instance, he wasn't getting what he wanted, and he and Freddie Young had a long talk, they put more sweat on me and then suggested I breathe more deeply and look into the camera.'

83

However, Barbara Cole believed that Lean's own interest in Christie went beyond the paternal. 'I noticed it during the scenes where she's having a mixed-up relationship with Komarovsky,' she said. 'I thought to myself, "He's really attracted to this woman."' But I was there.' Christie conceded, 'I felt he really did care for me, but that may be part of David's charm—to make people, particularly women, feel that.' However, she still insisted that she 'felt a closeness based on paternalism'.

Freddie Young had arrived in Spain to take over as director of photography after Lean fell out with Nicolas Roeg. The director had hired Roeg, his second-unit director on *Lawrence of Arabia*, after being unable to secure the services of Young, who won an Oscar for his photography on that previous film. The pair's disagreements started when Roeg complained that it was difficult to light Geraldine Chaplin in a flattering way. Then, in the first full week of February 1965, they were due to shoot the night-time scene in which Bolshevik demonstrators are mown down by dragoons charging on horses down the main street of Moscow. Roeg insisted that the residents would not look on from their balconies but stay indoors with the lights off, so the scene should be shot in virtual darkness. Lean was adamant that the multi-million-pound set should be shown off as much as possible, and in the argument that followed he fired Roeg. By this time, Young was available and flew out to Spain to take over.

For the sequence in which Lara, while looking for husband Pasha, meets Zhivago as thousands of rebel Russian troops return on foot from the front during the First World War, Lean made no secret of basing the action on American director King Vidor's 1925 picture *The Big Parade*. In the film, also set during the war, stars John Gilbert and Renee Adoree bid farewell to one another, with the actress seen in close-up as troops constantly move in the background towards the front. 'So it was a static figure against this flow of soldiers,' said Lean, 'and I thought, "God, that's marvellous, a tremendous sense of movement." I never forgot it. I copied it almost exactly in *Zhivago*.'

The massive horseback charge on a 'snow-covered lake' was actually shot back in Spain, near Madrid during the summer, on a field transformed by special-effects designer Eddie Fowlie, who used thousands of tons of crushed white marble dust flattened by steamrollers.

During a couple of rare moments of spare time during the long shoot, Christie socialized with Ken Annakin and his wife, who were in Madrid while the director was making *The Battle of the Bulge*, a war drama in contrast to the two comedies that Christie had made with him at the beginning of her film career.

In the last week of March 1965, some of the *Zhivago* cast and crew moved more than 2,000 miles away to the outer reaches of Finland to shoot scenes of real snow, which was in short supply in Spain. They flew to Helsinki and then on about 400 miles north to the lumber town of Joensuu, where headquarters were established, close to the Arctic Circle and just seventy-five miles from the Russian border, with temperatures ranging from 40 to 10 degrees below zero. For two weeks, they stayed there in the freezing cold with nothing to do but work or wait around while filming dramatic scenes on snow-swept plains and steppes. Omar Sharif was involved in most of the scenes, but Christie did not go. The Finnish-based scenes finished with Zhivago gazing through a frosted pane of glass, the picture dissolving into a field full of bright yellow daffodils, signalling a change in the season.

Back in Soria, the northern Spanish town where the next scene was to be shot in April, the cast and crew stayed in two hotels. Seven thousand daffodils imported from Holland had been planted there, with the idea that they would be covered by snow before they bloomed in the spring scenes. With no snow falling and unusually mild weather, the flowers had already shown signs of life in January, so they were dug up and potted. Suddenly, after the cast and crew's return to Spain, the snows arrived and the potted daffodils were taken out and put in place. Then, the snow began to melt and became patchy, so marble dust was sprinkled around liberally to supplement it.

It was also in Soria that designer John Box recreated the 'Ice Palace' at Varykino, the house in which Lara and Zhivago seek refuge before their enforced separation and in which Zhivago writes his love poem to her. Lean's inspiration for this set was a photograph of Captain Scott in the Antarctic, dead in a room with snow coming in through a hole in the roof, although film critics were to liken it to the cobwebbed sanctuary of Miss Havisham in his production of *Great Expectations*. Of more immediate concern, the lack of snow in Soria meant that special-effects supremo Eddie Fowlie once again had to move into action, using Polystyrene chips forced through a wood planing machine.

During boring moments spent while waiting to film in Soria, Christie confided to a journalist, 'Spain has been good for me because I was beginning to get a bit flash. You know what I mean? I was raising my voice in public and calling people *"Dahling!"* '

But Christie was unhappy that, during two weeks in Soria when filming schedules did not require her to be there, Lean forbade her to go away on a trip with boyfriend Don Bessant, who had flown to Spain to see her. 'The only time David's paternalism did not suit me,' she explained, 'was when I wanted to go off exploring Spain during a week or two when I wasn't needed. But he wanted to keep us under his wing, *in case.* Then I retreated like a sulky schoolgirl.'

Christie and Bessant became engaged in Spain during the summer of 1965. By then Bessant was a lithographer teaching at both Maidstone College of Art and St Martin's Art School, London. However, such was the publicity over the engagement that he returned to St Martin's to find himself sacked from that part-time job.

Despite their engagement and 'special relationship', as she described it, Christie made it clear that they had no plans to marry and voiced doubts about whether the relationship with Bessant would last. Asked about it in Madrid a month before filming finished on *Doctor Zhivago*, she said, 'I don't see myself getting married. I'm always serious when I start a new friendship, but not for long. I know it won't last. Honestly, I don't think I could ever give myself utterly to one man.' However, the couple appeared to be devoted to one another and Bessant regularly accompanied Christie on visits to her mother in Wales, at Christmas.

The final part of *Doctor Zhivago*'s nine-month shoot took place on the mammoth streets set constructed near Madrid airport, with filming finishing on 7 October. Christie was not sorry to see the end of the gruelling schedule and admitted, 'I didn't enjoy making the film . . . but the people in it were very pleasant. Geraldine Chaplin in particular has that rare quality of being liked by women as much as men—but somehow I felt awfully "out of it", which sounds daft! I was very alone and was glad when it was over.'

An exhausted Christie returned to London and the flat in the West Kensington/ Hammersmith area in which she lived by then with Bessant and many cats. They were surrounded by a mixture of modern furniture and Portobello Road antiques, with a huge Union Jack hanging in the front hall. 'I moved out of the attic I used to share with lots of my mates and took a new place,' she said. 'I was sort of brainwashed into it. "You're not still living there?" people said. So I moved.'

But fame and fortune, Christie insisted, had changed her little. 'The sudden amount of money I have been earning has not made much difference to my life,' she explained, 'except that it has allowed me to move into a very pleasant flat and I can furnish it and buy bits and pieces that catch my eye, without feeling guilty. I enjoy clothes, as long as they are not gimmicky, and, there again, this money means I can spoil myself a bit.' However, after filming *Doctor Zhavago*, Christie appeared in a television commercial for hair conditioner, claiming that she did so for the money, enabling her to clear a bank overdraft.

After several months back home with Bessant, Christie's views on marriage had not changed. 'I'm happy living the way I do,' she insisted, 'but I don't think I'm equipped for marriage and, until I begin to feel very strongly about it, there is no reason to go through with something I feel is so unnecessary. The only times I do start dreaming is when I get those occasional maternal pangs but, thank goodness, they leave me as quickly as they come.'

In Britain, an exhausted Christie had been able to take a rest from filming, catch up with her friends—all from outside the film world, mostly creative types—enjoy dancing to pop music at her favourite clubs, the Ad Lib and the Flamingo, and even visit her mother in Wales.

But Lean—who edited many reels of film while shooting *Doctor Zhivago*—had only two months to prepare the film for release so that it would qualify for nominations in the next Oscars ceremony. He supervised the final editing at MGM's Culver City Studios, from more than thirty-one hours of footage, so that the picture was ready for its world premiere at Loew's Capitol cinema, in New York, on 22 December and the Hollywood Paramount cinema a day later.

Lean also oversaw the composition of a musical score by Maurice Jarre, who had previously won an Oscar for his work on *Lawrence of Arabia*. One memorable legacy of *Doctor Zhivago* is 'Lara's Theme', played over the end titles and throughout the film. It has since been recorded by others who have enjoyed hits with it in instrumentals and a vocal version, under the title 'Somewhere My Love'. However, the tune, performed in the picture on the balalaika, a three-stringed Russian instrument, was written late in the day after it was discovered that a Russian folk song intended to be used was still in copyright.

When the 197-minute-long *Doctor Zhivago* was finally released, Lean was shocked to receive damning reviews from the American critics. Judith Crist wrote in the *New York Herald Tribune*, 'It is merely spectacular soap opera . . . For the Pasternak Lara—the epitome of sunlit femininity, human honesty and womanly devotion—Miss Christie would, from her previous roles, seem the perfect answer . . . But the vital Miss Christie is suddenly suffering, suffering in a strangely impassive fashion, wearing a gloomy expression from start to finish.'

Immediately after the New York premiere, fifteen minutes was cut from the film, MGM added $1 million to the promotional budget and Lean travelled around the globe to publicize the picture. Despite the critics' loathing for it, audiences flocked to see *Doctor Zhivago*, which eventually took more than

$200 million at box offices worldwide. Lean himself earned at least $10 million, more than all of his previous pictures put together had made him. The film itself was dubbed into twenty-two foreign-language versions, more than any other in MGM's history, surpassing *Gone with the Wind.*

The European premiere, attended by Princess Margaret and her then husband, Lord Snowdon, was at the Empire Theatre, Leicester Square, London, on 26 April 1966. Christie was one of the few to escape largely unscathed in the British critics' reviews. In the *Observer*, Kenneth Tynan followed his verdict on *Doctor Zhivago* by writing, 'But it is Julie Christie who dominates the film— smouldering, vulnerable and much better cast than she was in *Darling.* Her erotic scenes have an urgent warmth that few English actresses could rival.' After describing the picture as 'dull and vulgar', Dan Jacobson added in the *New Statesman*, 'Miss Christie's nose, it now occurs to me, is one of the redeeming features which I said earlier the film was without: it is quite the prettiest nose I've seen on the screen since Ingrid Bergman's.'

Nevertheless, little more than a week earlier, *Doctor Zhivago*, like *The Sound of Music*, won five Oscars at the American Academy Awards ceremony, although it failed to take the most important honours. In fact, Christie was on hand to receive the Best

Actress award for her performance in *Darling*; *Zhivago*, meanwhile, was acknowledged for its screenplay by Frederic Raphael, cinematography by Freddie Young, set design and art decoration by John Box, Terry Marsh and Dario Simom, costume design by Phyllis Dalton and music by Maurice Jarre. Lean was shocked not to land the Oscar for Best Director and *The Sound of Music* was named Best Picture.

*   *   *

With or without *Doctor Zhivago*, Christie was now hot property and already seeking to tackle the problem of keeping as much of her earnings as possible. In December 1965, two months after the filming of *Doctor Zhivago* was completed, she became involved in what ten years later was ruled illegal by the High Court and described as 'one of the most complex and elaborate tax avoidance schemes ever witnessed'.

In late 1965, Christie's earnings were predicted to total up to £475,000 over the next seven years, after expenses and her agent's commission were deducted. So in an attempt to avoid higher-rate tax she entered into an agreement with a company called Rosebroom, undertaking to serve it exclusively as an actress for seven years at a salary rising from £7,500 to £13,500 a year. Rosebroom could then effectively exploit her professional services by selling them to film companies, in the way that Joseph Janni had previously done. However, in this case, the balance of Christie's income went to a company that then paid specially set-up trusts, which in turn paid beneficiaries who included the actress herself.

This came about after Christie's agent, Olive Harding of London Artists, approached Stanley Gorrie, a partner in accountants Stanley Gorrie Whitson & Co and Stanley Gorrie & Partners, asking how to minimize her client's tax payments. The result was an 'open commercial trust scheme' invented by Timothy Jones, a Supreme Court solicitor. The details were sealed at an important meeting held in a suite at the Park Lane Grosvenor House Hotel, in London, on 22 December 1965. All those present followed a script carefully prepared by Jones, based on what had previously been agreed by all parties and becoming binding in law once the words were spoken.

Rosebroom was set up with an issued share capital of £2, held by the two directors of Stanley Gorrie Whitson & Co. Stanley Gorrie & Partners acted as 'financiers' in the scheme and three key trusts were set up. One of them, Black Nominees, eventually received $67\frac{1}{2}$ per cent of the profits in the form of a loan, with Christie benefiting from it. The remaining $32\frac{1}{2}$ per cent went to the seller of the scheme,

Stanley Gorrie & Partners, and its associates. The hotel meeting also resulted in banker's drafts totalling about £475,000, in account with merchant bank Knowsley & Co, being passed between half-a-dozen companies.

In 1975 a High Court judge remarked, 'I assume that Knowsley were in a position to lend £475,000 when they arrived but they departed without leaving any such sum on loan to anyone.' All those involved in the scheme were paid by or represented Christie or the financiers, except the taxpayer trustees. The loans were paid as capital sums, but the profits to be earned from the rights to the actress's services were income, not capital receipts. The transactions disguised the fact that the distribution of profits from the rights to Christie's services was the only effect of the documents—no one would pay that much real money for what Black had to offer. All of the £475,000 had disappeared. However, Mr Justice Templeman, in his ruling, emphasized that there was no suggestion of fraud. 'People take you over when you earn money, and you must just say "yes",' Christie explained later. 'I was made a test because I am so appalling at business.'

CHAPTER SEVEN

TEMPERATURES SOAR

Between her December 1965 financial arrangement being concluded and leaving London on 16 April the next year for the Oscars ceremony, Christie had another film to shoot. She was playing a dual role in French new-wave director François Truffaut's adaptation of Ray Bradbury's bizarre 1950s science-fiction novel *Fahrenheit 451*, set in a totalitarian future in which books are banned as reminders of a decadent past.

She starred, alongside Austrian actor Oskar Werner, as both Clarisse, the schoolteacher in an anti-intellectual society in which books are burned, and Linda, the dutiful wife of Montag (Werner), a loyal fireman who has never questioned his function of carrying out the burning, until he meets the uninhibited Clarisse. He returns home to find the equally unquestioning, gentle Linda absorbing the propaganda being broadcast on television. Soon he starts taking books home at night and reading them, but is eventually discovered by Linda, who denounces him to the authorities. As a result, Montag joins Clarisse—by now also recognized as a book lover and on the run—and in the woods on the outskirts of the city they join 'bookmen', who have committed the classics to memory in the hope of continuing the struggle against totalitarianism.

'It wasn't so much the story that attracted me as working with Truffaut, whom I admire enormously,' Christie explained. 'I would do anything to work with people I admire; I just trust them and go ahead. I am terribly flattered that François should choose me.'

Fahrenheit 451, Truffaut's only film in the English language, made at Pinewood Studios, west of London, had taken three-and-a-half years to come to fruition after the director bought the rights in mid-1962. French producers had considered the project too risky and American companies decided against it, until New York producer Lewis Allen agreed in 1963 to make it as an English-language film.

It took a further two years to find financial backing, which eventually came from the Music Corporation of America's London office. It was the first of its independent films to be distributed by Universal, which had previously refused to pay Christie $35,000 for *The War Lord*. She was now worth much more. The second picture in this deal, Charlie Chaplin's disappointing final film, *A Countess from Hong Kong*, started shooting at Pinewood shortly after the cameras began rolling on *Fahrenheit 451*, whose title referred to the temperature at which books were burned to ashes.

Truffaut had considered shooting in Brasilia, Stockholm, Toronto, Chicago or Meudon, in France, but decided on Pinewood. The director of photography was Nicolas Roeg, who had been sacked by David Lean on the set of *Doctor Zhivago*. On this film, he was responsible for the distinctive sombre images on screen. He and Christie were to work together again on *Far from the Madding Crowd*, *Petulia* and, after Roeg switched to directing, *'Don't Look Now'*.

With a budget of £500,000, filming of *Fahrenheit 451* was due to start on Monday, 10 January 1966, but the insurance company's doctor pronounced Christie too exhausted after her long stint on *Doctor Zhivago*, so the first day's shoot was put back a week. Christie also had to have a wisdom tooth removed. As a result, Oskar Werner returned to Berlin and Paris to dub himself in German and French for his starring role in *The Spy Who Came in from the Cold*.

By Wednesday of that week, Universal had decided that filming must go ahead on the next day, but shooting schedules had to be amended and Christie did not film her first scene until 31 January. In it an old woman chooses to die with her burning books, rather than be left without them, and commits suicide like a Buddhist monk. A surrealistic part of the sequence called for Christie to wear the same clothes as the woman, stand in the middle of the books, strike a match and collapse in slow motion. 'Julie was jittery,' Truffaut recorded in his diary, 'but she came through it well.'

It was another four days before Christie appeared on set again, when shooting started on all her scenes as television-watching Linda, wearing a long, silky wig. Truffaut had instructed costume designer Tony Walton to dress Linda in 'glossy materials', as in Carole Lombard's gown in *To Be or Not to Be*, whereas Clarisse's clothes should be made of 'dull and unglossy' materials.

Truffaut resolved to film Christie in profile while playing Linda, highlighting her straight nose, turned-back upper lip and wide mouth. After the first day's shooting on the set of Montag and Linda's apartment, Truffaut noted, 'Julie Christie is going to be wonderful, as easy to work on as Jeanne Moreau or Françoise Dorleac; like them, she's trusting, never fusses and never asks theoretical questions like: "What is She feeling when She says so and so and this and that." When the 'rushes' of film shot came through, Truffaut pronounced, 'Julie Christie is superb. She uses her eyes to cast wonderful stylized looks, she can do anything. Unfortunately, the role of Linda being what it is, I am using only part of her talent.'

Most of Christie's scenes as Linda took less than two weeks to film. To Truffaut's delight, she made the character more sympathetic and human than Mildred from the novel, on whom she was based. After several more days shooting other scenes featuring Werner, the director handed over Stage E at Pinewood to Charlie Chaplin for a ship's ballroom sequence in his film. Truffaut had been under pressure from Chaplin's crew for almost a week to complete the apartment scenes.

Week six of filming, halfway through the schedule, began with Christie switching to the character of Clarisse. For this she had short hair and Truffaut filmed her face-on, not in profile. The second day of filming on the set of Clarisse's cellar, where she and Montag burn some papers, was marred by an argument between Truffaut and Werner—not their first. Werner wanted to touch Christie's arm and shoulders, and wanted her to look at him after a certain line of his, but Truffaut was adamant that there should be no romance between Montag and Clarisse. He considered that an adulterous affair had no place in science fiction. 'On several occasions,' wrote the director, 'out of sheer battle-fatigue, I have allowed Oskar [to] play a scene his way (protecting myself with the means to get round it in the editing), but I will not have him interfering in Julie Christie's and Cyril Cusack's performances by suggesting bits of business to them the moment my back is turned.

Werner had previously argued with Truffaut

about the way in which Cusack, as the menacing fire station captain, was handling a flame-thrower in the scene involving the old woman's suicide. From now on, the pair spoke to each other to say only what was necessary to complete the rest of the scenes in the film. Production manager Ian Lewis believed that the root of the disagreement between director and star was the failure of Werner to admit a phobia of his before shooting started. 'Oskar didn't tell anybody that he was terrified of fire,' explained Lewis. 'They clashed because of that, really. It was a very deceitful thing to have done. He didn't like using the flame-thrower and, when we came to the first shot where he had to use it, he wouldn't do it. We had to get round it and put a stuntman in scenes where possible, and Oskar had to wear a mask, which made life very difficult.'

Scottish actor Tom Watson, who had a small role in the picture, also recalled the shooting of *Fahrenheit 451* as being rather unhappy:

Most of my scenes were with Oskar. At one point, we were sitting in chairs at the side of the set. I tried to make conversation, but he was totally monosyllabic. The only thing he said to me was, 'Have you got the right time?' I think he was bored, and he was very brusque with me, an unknown fellow actor. During filming, the only note I ever heard Truffaut give, through an interpreter, was,

101

'Make sure they all have their watches on the correct wrist.' There seemed to be no team feeling on the picture. Truffaut only spoke in French, which is a big barrier.

Ian Lewis recalled:

The biggest problem was that Truffaut had never worked with a big team and he only spoke French. He usually made his pictures with a maximum of 20 people, with everybody doing everything—it was very much a family affair when Truffaut directed a movie. For *Fahrenheit 451*, he had an American woman who acted as an interpreter. Most of the crew didn't speak French or like going through the interpreter, so they went off and did things themselves without discussion, such as colour schemes on particular sets. I'd show Truffaut the next set we were due to shoot on and he would hold his hands up in horror because it wasn't what he wanted and it would have to be changed.

The director's relationship with Christie, who could speak French, remained happy, although Lewis recalled one problem that he shielded from Truffaut. 'She would arrive at the studio nearly always late and very scruffy— very scruffy,' he explained. 'I think she was burning the candle at both ends. She used to come in looking appalling and her hair had to be completely redone every day. I'd have make-up saying, "How are we going to get her ready on time?" But we tried to keep it from Truffaut so that he didn't have to worry about it.'

Truffaut was unstinting in his admiration for Christie during filming. 'Her interpretation is so consistently right,' Truffaut wrote in his diary on 1 March, 'that my work is limited to stopping her from using too much movement or too little, and to getting her to slow down her performance by splitting it up to an almost exaggerated extent—one broad gesture instead of two small ones, a look broken down into three stages, expressions that give serenity to her face without it being necessary to smile, and so on.'

The director had encouraged Christie to play Linda and Clarisse as almost identical women so that the contrast in their respectively accepting and rebellious attitudes was more dramatic, showing what could happen to the same woman if she allowed herself to be brainwashed. During filming, Truffaut noticed Christie's insecurity, restlessness and ability to remain oblivious to all that was happening around her between 'takes', saying to herself the lines she was about to speak in front of the camera. 'Julie dislikes her body from head to foot,' he wrote, 'her bosom because she thinks it's too flat, her legs because they're too thin. She has had the right instinct where they are concerned, however, for instead of trying to divert attention to another part of her body, she has chosen to display her legs a great deal by wearing mini-skirts and dresses.'

Looking at the 'rushes' of daily footage, Truffaut realized that Christie had a small head compared with Werner's large one. So he always tried to separate them in scenes and shoot her close-ups closer than his. Some exterior filming was done in Roehampton, south-west London, and downstream on the Thames. The firehouse and Clarisse's classroom were filmed in the studio, as were interiors of the Paris monorail, where Clarisse and Montag meet. Exteriors of the monorail were shot in Château-neuf-sur-Loire, near Orléans, when filming switched to France in the last week of March, before a final two weeks' work back at Pinewood and nearby locations. Christie finished her last scene on her birthday, 14 April, and two days later she and Werner left for the Oscars ceremony. She won an award, of course, but he—nominated for *Ship of Fools*—lost out to Lee Marvin, star of *Cat Ballou*.

Working with Truffaut had been a happy experience for Christie, in whom she found a soulmate. 'I remember the both of us were so shy we could hardly talk to each other,' she recalled. 'I gave him an old electric train set and we'd play with the trains in an effort to try and communicate in some way.' Camera operator Alex Thomson, who had previously worked for two weeks in the same job as a stand-in when Christie was filming *Darling*, recalled, 'She liked Truffaut very much and got on well with everybody.'

Director Alan Lovell filmed Christie on and off set during the making of *Fahrenheit 451* for a documentary short entitled *Star*, intended to show the nature of stardom as epitomized by the actress. It also included clips from *Billy Liar!*, *Doctor Zhivago* and *A for Andromeda*, as well as film of the *Darling* premiere. 'As Julie Christie appears to have nothing whatsoever to say in the interviews, and the commentary labours under a series of trite observations about the star system, the result is not exactly inspiring,' wrote one critic.

When *Fahrenheit 451* was poorly reviewed after being premiered at the Venice Film Festival on 7 September 1966, Universal decided to give the picture a limited release in Britain to 'specialized audiences'. Truffaut knew from the outset of filming that the characters were not strong, but he believed this was compensated for by the extraordinary situation. Ray Bradbury confessed to 'mixed reactions' to this adaptation of his novel, and Christie's next film received the same response from many critics at the time, although it was to prove more enduring.

CHAPTER EIGHT

HARDY'S HEROINE

As Bathsheba Everdene, at the centre of the action in *Far from the Madding Crowd*, Christie was playing another independent woman. This time she was seen against the backdrop of Thomas Hardy's Wessex, a panoramic landscape captured beautifully by director of photography Nicolas Roeg, and John Schlesinger, the director to whom Christie returned.

Schlesinger's admirable but flawed attempt to bring Hardy's nineteenth-century novel to the screen saw Christie teaming up with Terence Stamp, Alan Bates and Peter Finch as Bathsheba's suitors. Sergeant Troy (Stamp) is the dashing soldier who steals Bathsheba's heart and wins her hand in marriage before apparently committing suicide; Boldwood (Finch) the rich but older and dull landowner who realizes that his money alone cannot buy love; and Gabriel Oak (Alan Bates) the faithful labourer who watches on as his employer considers these other men as potential husbands.

Just as the idea for *Darling* had surfaced while shooting *Billy Liar!*, putting a Thomas Hardy novel on screen was suggested to John

106

Schlesinger and Joseph Janni by film editor Jim Clark during post-production work on *Darling*. Although not very enthusiastic at first, Schlesinger eventually conceded that he wanted his next film to be 'something more romantic about another age' and felt that nineteenth-century England was the perfect setting.' Recalling Clark's remarks, he approached MGM with it, but the studio responded with the idea of doing a remake of its 1924 silent film version of another Hardy novel, *Tess of the D'Urbervilles.*

Schlesinger and Janni stuck to their guns, although the director was unsure about whether Christie would be too closely associated with the Swinging Sixties character of Diana Scott in *Darling* to carry off the role of Bathsheba. He even considered approaching Vanessa Redgrave. Holding on to the resolution they had demonstrated in trying to get *Darling* off the ground with Christie in the lead role, the pair decided to keep faith with her. MGM finally agreed to a film version of *Far from the Madding Crowd* on condition that it was a blockbuster, supplying a $4 million budget to ensure this. However, this conflicted with Schlesinger and Janni's original notion of the picture as being small and intimate.

Filming in the Dorset countryside began in the late summer of 1966, when most of the English public were celebrating their football

107

team's victory in the World Cup. *Far from the Madding Crowd* did not match that triumph, although its visual delights have made it worth further viewings on television over the years. During eight months of filming, the seasons changed from summer to autumn and on to winter and spring. Nicolas Roeg's spectacular cinematography, from panning shots of hills, cliffs and sea to images of sowing, sheep-dipping and harvesting, formed a backdrop for the characters in the same way that David Lean had used the landscape in *Doctor Zhivago* and his previous epic, *Lawrence of Arabia*.

Magical moments include scenes of Bathsheba disappearing on a pony-and-trap into a hill-mist; a flock of sheep, dogs and a shepherd in a field of golden stubble; a small boy walking next to a sunlit meadow learning his catechism, with a white horse rolling in the grass and huge trees towering behind him; a sea-level shot of Troy swimming away from land to his presumed suicide; Oak rescuing Bathsheba's harvested crops in a storm; his sheep being run over a cliff by an inexperienced sheepdog; and Bathsheba and Troy's wedding-harvest festivities that leave all the farmhands drunk.

During the long shooting schedule, which Christie left only to attend the Paris premiere of *Fahrenheit 451*, she endured moments when two of her greatest assets—her face and breast—were threatened. In a sequence known as the sword-dance scene, shot at Maiden Castle, near Dorchester, Sergeant Troy had to remove a caterpillar from the front of Bathsheba's dress with his sword. 'What you saw on screen was actually my hand holding the sword,' said swordmaster Derek Ware, who trained Stamp and played a corporal in the film. 'We affixed a pin to the point of the sword and attempted to skewer the caterpillar on the end of it, but it wouldn't work. I couldn't actually strike her on the mammary gland, so we built a pad into the bosom of her costume. As the caterpillar got to a certain point, I had to lunge at it, but I missed the caterpillar and, as I struck at the padded brassière, the caterpillar instinctively rolled itself into a ball round the point of the sword.'

Immediately afterwards in the same scene, Stamp had to use his sword to lop off an 'untidy' curl of Christie's hair, actually a wig. 'I trained him to do the cut from a certain angle,' recalled Ware. 'But, when it came to filming, they wanted him to do it from another angle so that a flash of the dying sunlight would catch the sword. As a result, he biffed her in the face with the sword and, if you watch carefully, you can see her rear back at the moment of impact. She had a very small abrasion on her face.'

Many of Christie's scenes were set in Bathsheba's farmhouse, in reality in

Bloxworth, between Dorchester and Poole. She had to stand her 5 ft 3 in frame on a box for some of them, such as the sword-dance sequence with Stamp. 'Julie was petite,' recalls Ware. 'She was fragile, like a little doll, whereas on screen she looked formidable, very much a 1960s chick, totally in control of herself and everything else. One has come to realize since that she wasn't. It must have been terribly overwhelming for her. She must have been desperately insecure because the whole world was looking at her and everyone wanted to interview her. She was the Madonna of her time.'

Freddie Jones, who played Cainy Hall, recalled, 'Julie has always been quite modest about her talents and I remember her being overwhelmed when confronted by certain members of the Royal Shakespeare Company who were in *Far from the Madding Crowd.* She lacked confidence in her own talent.'

Even worse, Christie had to face the wrath of the usually calm John Schlesinger when she arrived late for the wedding-harvest barn dance, shot in a huge tithe barn at Abbotsbury, west of Weymouth. The company included among its musicians Dave Swarbrick, later to gain recognition as a member of the folk group Fairport Convention. Brian Rawlinson, who played farm labourer Matthew Moon, said:

The place was packed with people, all the

locals from around the area as farmers, labourers and neighbours, the regular actors like Freddie Jones, Fiona Walker and myself who in the screenplay, as workers on the Wetherby Farm, acted as a kind of chorus, and all the production crew. For some reason, our transport had been delayed and, although we were late, we all seemed to be in a skittish and frivolous mood.

The first set-up was a big, wide, general shot of the whole barn with a group of us ready to begin the country dance, which had been choreographed the day before. My job was to lead it off with Julie as my partner. But no Julie! It occurred to us that John Schlesinger was, quite rightly, not pleased. In fact, he was in a foul temper, which is so unusual in a man who is always so placid, genial and good-humoured. I've known John for a long time but, with a long, busy and complicated sequence to cover, his attitude was not surprising.

As the atmosphere grew tenser and tenser, we ail sobered up, of course. Then, finally, Julie did arrive, apologized quietly and took her place in front of me, ready to start. John bore down on her and gave her hell. The huge space was silent. My proximity to this tirade was extremely embarrassing because I felt—we all did— that we were all at fault and Julie was getting the brunt of it. To be so publicly

111

humiliated, as the star of the film, I expected her to either burst into tears or rush off the set, or both. But she did neither. She simply lowered her head, blushed slightly and stood her ground. John stomped off, gave the orders for a rehearsal and some general directions, and that was that.

As the amazing Dave Swarbrick struck up on his fiddle, I took Julie's hand, ready for the first part of the dance, and squeezed it for comfort. 'I'm sorry about that,' I whispered. 'So am I,' she murmured back. And off we clomped. We were playing country folk, after all. I don't know whether such *sangfroid* animates the matador when faced with the bull, but her calm stopped the animal anger dead in its tracks.

A bigger problem had to be tackled when Christie arrived on set for a scene in which sheep were being injected in the fields. 'She said, "Good morning, what are you going to do about this?" as she pointed to a cold sore on her lip,' recalled director of photography Nicolas Roeg. 'We got the make-up and the nurse to put new "skin" over the cold sore and stuck a lock of hair from Julie's wig to it. Then, we used a wind machine to make it appear as if her hair were being blown across her face by the wind and overlaid the relevant sound effects afterwards. I found it quite amusing that the publicity people used that shot of Julie on one of the posters.'

Although the film's stars rented properties during shooting, many of the supporting cast stayed at two hotels in Weymouth. That coastal town was where everyone converged at the end of each day's filming. Christie mixed with just a small group from the cast and crew, enjoying the company of Freddie Jones, Peter Finch, Fiona Walker—who had been at the Central School of Speech and Drama with her—Nicolas Roeg and focus puller Tony Richmond. 'Our salvation was a bistro on the water in Weymouth that stayed open for us well into the night,' recalled Jones of the long shoot. 'We had quite riotous nights, but Julie didn't stay out too late because she was the star and had a busy schedule.' Finch was sometimes joined by his daughter, Diana, or a girlfriend, and Christie's partner, Don Bessant, was also a visitor to Dorset during filming.

Jones also remembered Christie, Finch and Walker joining him, his wife, the actress Jennifer Heslewood, and their newborn son to look round a mine sweeper at Portland Bill. Other members of the cast formed their own social groups. 'The Mill Set', as they became known, spent much of their free time at Alan Bates's rented mill house at Upwey. They included Brian Rawlinson, Andrew Robertson and Denise Coffey, who enjoyed playing Pergolesi and Nina Simone records and 'performing' on a pianola there. 'Every so often, we'd go over to John Schlesinger's place for lunch and tell him all the gossip, which he loved,' said Brian Rawlinson.

Each night Christie would return to a rented farm cottage at Osmington Mills. On a dark and misty 5 November, recalled Rawlinson, she invited the cast and crew over for a fireworks party, complete with large bonfire and hot buffet. 'Friends had come down from London and I remember Bob Powell [actor Robert Powell] and I making a great go of it with the fire and the Guy, leaping about with sparklers and generally making idiots of ourselves. But it was a social occasion and gossip with Julie was general and not important. For the most part, she kept herself very much to herself and we only met during the filming in the way of work.'

But within her small group Christie revealed a discontent with the press that soon led her to give few interviews. 'She used to get furious with writers who so edited their articles that it made her look as though she had said things that she hadn't,' said Freddie Jones. 'She received letters from all over the world, from people like bishops, attacking her for saying things she hadn't in fact said.'

Working with his former girlfriend was no problem for Terence Stamp, who was by then in a long-term relationship with legendary model Jean Shrimpton. 'Passion was confined to the celluloid,' Stamp recalled. 'As Bathsheba and Troy Julie and Terry were inspiring lyrics, however—the Kinks songster, Ray Davies, included our names in his "Waterloo Sunset".'

The left-handed actor was more concerned with learning to ride a horse and being taught by Derek Ware to use a military sabre in his right hand, because cavalry divisions in the 1860s accepted only right-handed soldiers. Stamp had an unhappy time during filming, citing differences with John Schlesinger and the fact that he had spent time perfecting a Dorset accent, only to be told by the director—on hearing the divergent vowels of his cast—that the stars would not be required to use it. More unhappiness followed for Stamp, with Shrimpton leaving him before the royal premiere of *Far from the Madding Crowd*, at the Marble Arch Odeon in September 1967.

The film had little success outside Britain. Its greatest asset was Nicolas Roeg's photography of the vast landscape, filmed in muted tones, but screenwriter Frederic Raphael's compression of the novel omitted complexities in the characters of Bathsheba, Oak, Troy and Boldwood. Some thought that Christie was miscast in the role of Bathsheba.

A lukewarm response from American audiences after the film's New York premiere a month later led MGM to cut the running time in cinemas there by twenty minutes. One result was that it finished with the happy

115

scenes of Bathsheba's marriage to Gabriel. However, these were actually tempered by a subsequent, final sequence in which the couple exchange glances at home one afternoon before the camera pans to show a music box with a figure of a soldier dressed in a scarlet and black uniform, given to her as a wedding-day present by her dead first husband, Troy.

The cuts were made without consulting Schlesinger, who had attended the New York premiere and who himself gauged that the film was too long for cinemagoers there. He complained to MGM, insisting that he could edit the film for general release in the United States without any missing footage being noticed. However, the studio, determined to finish with a happy ending, was adamant that the music-box sequence should remain on the cutting-room floor.

The critics, too, had mixed feelings about *Far from the Madding Crowd*. Charles Champlin, of the *Los Angeles Times*, highlighted an unevenness in the stars' performances, praising Peter Finch as Boldwood and adding, 'Julie Christie, whom I love as an actress, was indomitably contemporary as the Hardy heroine. Finch assumed the style, mannerisms and look of the Hardy character, but he never seemed to be acting. He was of that period, with strength, sensitivity, and every nuance realized.'

However, Christie managed to give a

charisma to her character that ensured audiences would not tire of it, despite being on screen for most of the film's 169 minutes. She did confess three decades later, 'It was actually quite an authoritative role—she knew how to get what she wanted—but I don't think I played her right.'

Schlesinger himself later admitted, 'We didn't adapt the novel with sufficient freedom. Although Hardy's setting is marvellous, his drama when distilled on film just doesn't work.' His praise for two of the stars also highlighted his reservations about some of the others. Talking about Peter Finch, Schlesinger said, 'I feel that he and Alan Bates gave absolutely wonderful performances. Some of the other performances in the film were uneven . . . In Peter and Alan I had two screen actors trained in the theatre with the dimension needed for Boldwood and Gabriel Oakes [sic].'

Schlesinger was resolved to leave costume dramas alone for a while, and Christie did the same, opting to step back into the present era, whose sense of liberation she was seen to embody.

CHAPTER NINE

MODERN GIRL

From the period drama of *Far from the Madding Crowd*, Christie moved firmly back into the 1960s. She was one of a dozen celebrities of the era to be featured in the documentary film *Tonite Let's All Make Love in London*, which captured the mood of the capital in this exciting time with a montage of pop music, art and political protest.

Christie was one of British cinema's brightest new stars and very much a child of the new generation, who believed anything was possible and sought to throw out the old conventions. She had also gained international recognition, as had British pop stars such as the Beatles and the Rolling Stones. This placed Britain—and, in particular, London—at the centre of the Swinging Sixties, and the year 1967 proved to be one of the decade's most interesting. 'Underground' groups such as the psychedelia pioneers Pink Floyd were breaking through, the Beatles released their *Sergeant Pepper's Lonely Hearts Club Band* concept album and Procul Harum hit the number one spot in the singles chart with their hallucinogenic 'A Whiter Shade of Pale'.

The release that year of *Tonite Let's All*

Make Love in London—a title taken from a line of Allen Ginsberg's poem *Who'd Be Kind To*—could not have been more timely. Produced and directed by Peter Whitehead, who also scripted and photographed it, the picture's impressionistic view of life in 1960s London began with a ten-minute sequence entitled 'Pop Concerto for Film', with original music by Pink Floyd. The rest of the picture was divided into sections featuring different aspects of 'swinging' Britain, starting tongue-in-cheek with the Changing of the Guard, which symbolized the shift away from tradition and the loss of the British Empire.

Other highlights included shots of mini-skirted girls dancing and novelist Edna O'Brien talking about the morality of the modern woman in 'Dolly Girls'; actress Vanessa Redgrave at an anti Vietnam War rally singing an unaccompanied song from Castro's Cuba in 'Protest'; an interview with Mick Jagger of the Rolling Stones in 'It's All Pop Music'; others with Alan Aldridge and David Hockney in 'Pop Art'; and scenes of Playboy Bunny Girls arriving in London in 'As Scene from the USA'.

Christie contributed to the 'Film Stars' sequence, questioning her own superficiality and confessing her need for 'close relationships'. In the same section, actor Michael Caine declares that the new society might be trading 'our morals for a mass of cultural pottage'. On the film's release in November 1967, Ann Pacey wrote in the *Sun* that these two film stars' interviews were 'so unilluminating and incoherent that they are actually very funny'.

Perhaps the feverish visual images of the film revealed the truth that much of this apparently happy new society was living for the moment, with future penalties to pay for its new freedoms. There were hints, too, that in the real world another society existed far removed from the gloss and glamour. The 'real world' of American bombs being dropped on Vietnam was itself portrayed in the documentary.

By the time *Tonite Let's All Make Love in London* received its premiere at the New York Film Festival in September 1967 and in the capital city of its title two months later, Christie had made her next film, *Petulia*, her first to be shot in America. It was the latest picture by new-wave director Richard Lester, an American who had made his name in Britain. He was a writer for the Goons on radio, before moving to television to direct Spike Milligan and Peter Sellers in shows such as *A Show Called Fred* and *Idiot Weekly, Price 2d.* He then used his surrealistic style in the Beatles' films *A Hard Day's Night* and *Help!*, as well as *The Knack . . . and how to get it*, which caught the atmosphere of the Swinging Sixties and the widening generation gap.

Originally another American director, Robert Altman, then still trying to find success in feature films, was due to make *Petulia*, which was based on the novel *Me and the Arch Kook Petulia*, by Los Angeles dentist John Haase. One of Altman's collaborators, Barbara Turner, wrote a screenplay, but Altman eventually passed on the rights in it to Raymond Wagner—who went on to produce the film, his first—as part of a deal that allowed the director to make a television series that, in the event, never reached the screen.

Wagner sent Turner's script to Lester, who did not like it, but read the book, which he hated. Lester said:

I thought it was all nonsense, false high-spiritedness, a comedy with people I disliked. I decided to pass on it. But, for some reason it began to get to me. I kept thinking, 'Why am I so angry about this? Why don't I just forget it?' At that point, I was about to shoot *How I Won the War* and I was very concerned about things that were changing in American society, very much for the worse, since I had left in the early 1950s. I began to consider what I was angry about. This was an American subject and one of the few that had got to me, because I had turned down all the others to make British or European subjects. I began to think, if I were to make this kind of film, what would it and the characters be like?

With the idea of switching the story to San Francisco and taking out the comedy elements, Lester set to work on some research with Charles Wood, who had written the screenplays for his films *The Knack*, *Help!* and *How I Won the War*. Lester recalled:

We spent a week wandering around San Francisco in 1966 and Charles wrote a series of reflections, almost a diary, based on what we did and saw and watched on television, and what attitudes we encountered. It was a complete stream of consciousness, as you write an unstructured diary. Charles wrote 60 to 70 pages, and I thought, 'There really is something.' We then worked back to the original material, looking at what we really needed and what seemed to ring true, because I didn't believe the book's characters would exist and I didn't care about them. I wanted to make a film that reflected my feelings of going back to America for the first time in 15 years, the beginnings of the Vietnam War and how I felt that world had changed from the one I grew up in, with that sense of casual violence that seemed to be permeating the society.

To ensure authentic American dialogue,

Lester then drafted in Lawrence B. Marcus to write the screenplay. Marcus's own experience of divorce also helped to make it a script that reflected a new feeling of disillusionment. Lester recalled:

> We were lucky that we turned up in San Francisco in 1966, which was the beginning of the hippy, flower-power, rockband scene. We observed that and its innocence. By the time we returned to start the final draft with Larry Marcus, which was a four-week job, what was fascinating was how that innocence had turned into cynicism, the racketeering in drugs and the sham of people who drove into town in their three-piece suits and changed into their hippy beads and put a flower behind their ear and then, at the end of the day, got back into their Ford Mustangs and drove out again.

So, with Warner Brothers of America backing the film, Christie played brazen English girl Petulia Danner, who cheats on her psychologically weak but violent husband, David (Richard Chamberlain), by having an affair with divorcé surgeon Archie (George C. Scott). As the story unfolds, the strength of Christie's character compared with that played by Chamberlain soon emerges.

As a backdrop, Lester portrays a modern-media society, with the countryside around

San Francisco being overrun by signboards and film crews making television commercials, the city populated by those of the topless, go-go generation featured in *Tonite Let's All Make Love in London.* Meanwhile, news from Vietnam filters through Archie's television, whose moving wallpaper is constant in the background of scenes.

Christie was cast in the title role of Petulia as a result of conversations between Lester and producer Wagner in the early stages of pre-production. Lester explained:

Apart from the fact that she had a screen presence and an extraordinary beauty, she's not an obvious realist. Petulia was always wanting so much that she was throwing away the 60 per cent that she *could* have. She helps to destroy her husband because she keeps expecting him to be phenomenal and telling him he must be phenomenal. In essence, he's a man with feet of clay and both hidden and open problems, and she's making it worse. She's also trying to force Archie to be something that *he* couldn't be.

She is unrealistically romanticizing life and I felt there was a quality about Julie that could produce that for us. She's not a kitchen-sink actress, not someone you would always associate with realism. She has that ethereal quality that comes partly from the beauty, but also she has within her an

124

extraordinary, unfettling nervousness. That is the essence of Petulia, the mercurial switches and changes, which the pedantic people of this world find exasperating.

So the kooky American woman of the original book was turned into a distraught English one. However, Lester had to fight hard to get the actors he wanted alongside her. He cast aside James Garner as the surgeon, despite the actor having been lined up by producer Wagner, as well as Frank Sinatra and Paul Newman, before settling on George C. Scott, whose film career had until then been undistinguished. Seeing him on television and the New York stage convinced Lester that he was right for the role. 'I absolutely adored his work,' explained Lester. 'If you're going to cast a man who is weak, you cast a strong actor. If you cast a weak actor playing a weak man, you get a boring performance. But, if you get a strong, really gutsy performer playing this man, you still have an underlying tension in it. George is the finest performer I've ever worked with.'

When Lester told Warner Brothers that he wanted Richard Chamberlain to play Petulia's husband, the studio insisted that he must not be hired. Although the actor had achieved heart-throb status in the title role of the American television series *Dr Kildare*, he also had a handful of unimpressive films behind him and a monumental stage flop with the musical *Breakfast at Tiffany's*. Standing firm, Lester eventually won the battle. 'Richard was an extraordinarily handsome man and the sexuality that he brought seemed to be correct for the part,' explained the director. 'I thought Richard and Julie fitted well together as a couple.'

Lester added a supporting cast of Joseph Cotten as Petulia's overbearing father-in-law and Shirley Knight as the surgeon's ex-wife. In addition to a score by John Barry, music of the era was represented by the inclusion of live performances by Janis Joplin, the Grateful Dead and others.

Two familiar faces to Christie on her arrival for filming in San Francisco were director of photography Nicolas Roeg, who had previously worked with her on *Fahrenheit 451* and *Far from the Madding Crowd*, and Tony Walton, the production and costume designer from *Fahrenheit 451.*

One problem during filming was the difference in acting styles between Christie and George Scott. He was a one-take actor, whereas Christie took time to get into the mood of scenes and often needed up to half-a-dozen takes. Lester solved this by filming the pair separately where possible. He explained:

Because she is somewhat insecure, Julie needs time to build into a scene. She liked a lot of rehearsal. It's odd because George, who was a theatre actor, was the most instinctive actor I've ever seen and got very bored after three or four takes, whereas Julie began to come into her own after five or six takes. It was a very difficult balance to keep both of them happy. I would do all George's close-ups first and then come round and cover Julie later so that she had time to practise while the camera was on her back. I took George's best bits early, giving Julie time to get comfortable. By the time she was ready, we were concentrating more on her than on him. Throughout the production, Julie was a good team player. Anything that we wanted her to do she did, willingly, with good grace and good spirit.

The director also allowed Christie to develop the role as she went along. 'There's nothing hard and fast with Dick Lester,' she said during filming. 'Petulia's character is evolving all the time.' However, her performance was not at its best in the scenes where she was called on to be wild and zany.

Lester was adamant that David Danner's attack on his wife need not be filmed—only the results of the violence had to be shown. He stamped his own mark on the film, surprising no one with the use of his jump-cut technique and 'smash and grab' raids on the San Francisco streets, a style previously seen in *The*

Knack . . . and how to get it. The film crew hid in the crowds and shot, using several cameras, as the stars walked among the public. Some filming was done in Sausalito, outside San Francisco, where Christie was staying on a houseboat, and some across the Mexican border, in Tijuana.

The picture received a critical mauling, and when it was chosen as America's official entry at the 1968 Cannes Film Festival its misfortunes continued. The screening was affected by the spread of riots and strikes that had started on the streets of Paris. When the violence arrived in Cannes, the police baton-charged demonstrators outside the main festival venue. Although *Petulia* was second-favourite to win the coveted top prize of the Palme D'Or, Lester decided to withdraw from the festival, along with other film-makers.

Christie returned to Europe and producer Joseph Janni to film the melodrama *In Search of Gregory*, although that proved to be another disappointment. A British-Italian co-production, filmed in Geneva and Rome, and at studios in London, it starred Christie as Swiss financier's daughter Catherine, an independent, cosmopolitan beauty who is attracted to Gregory (Canadian actor Michael Sarrazin), her much married father's house-guest from San Francisco. She has never met him, but on being invited to her father's fifth wedding, in Geneva, is intrigued by his description of this tall, handsome, 'likeable maniac'. At Geneva airport, she sees a poster of an auto-ball champion and he becomes the embodiment of her fantasies.

John Hurt also starred, as Catherine's neurotic brother, Daniel, displaying an openly incestuous love for his sister and a resulting fear of all women, who joins his father in weaving tales of Gregory. Catherine and the audience are left asking whether this man really exists, until on arriving at Geneva airport to return home to Rome she eventually meets the auto-ball player from the poster, quietly picks him up and goes with him to a hotel room to fulfil her fantasy—only to have it destroyed when he speaks and reveals himself to be a German medical student. The real Gregory had, ironically, been in Rome searching for Catherine, who was his fantasy woman. They pass at the airport without seeing one another.

In Search of Gregory was the first feature film by director Peter Wood, who had a distinguished background in the West End theatre with plays such as Harold Pinter's *The Birthday Party*, Peter Shaffer's *Five Finger Exercise* and Joe Orton's *Loot*, and the picture had a taut, psychological screenplay by Tonino Guerra and his mistress, Lucille Laks. Guerra had co-scripted, with Italian director Michelangelo Antonioni, the 1966 film *Blow-Up*, which explored the differences between

129

fantasy and reality against a swinging London backdrop. This seemed a natural progression—almost *'Darling* meets *Blow-Up'*.

Christie had been signed up to star in *In Search of Gregory* before Wood was hired. The director recalled more than thirty years later:

I was the novice. Jo Janni said to me one Saturday at lunch, 'If Chelsea win today, you can direct this film. And they did. *In Search of Gregory* was a difficult piece because the writers' respective styles were quite different from one another. They might have had a wonderful collaboration in bed, but it didn't work so well on the page. Tonino's scripts with Antonioni, such as *L'Avventura*, always had a philosophical overtone about people in them disappearing or whether they existed at all, whereas Lucille was much more practical. So they were pulling against one another. If Gregory had been a total fantasy, simply a face on a poster but not a person, the film would have worked much better.

At the time, I had great faith in Tonino. After all, he was world-famous. When you have a script from someone who's worked with Antonioni, you're just thrilled. It was a chance for me, and I felt I missed it. Once the film began to cut together, I could see what was wrong with it, that it was too concrete. Nowadays, it's not necessary to explain everything and rationalize. That is the legacy of Antonioni and those great Italian film-makers. Afterwards, very gradually, you began to get other scripts of the same kind.

Plans to film in Paris were abandoned because of the May riots in France that had already led Richard Lester to leave the Cannes Film Festival. So the story was based in Geneva instead. Wood's recollections of shooting *In Search of Gregory* became dominated by the thrill of making his feature debut and working with a star as big as Christie. 'She was an extremely glamorous, Sixties lady,' he recalled. 'If you look back at the publicity pictures, you'll see her wearing those Sixties skirts and showing those wonderful knees. I have nothing but glamorous and exciting memories of the whole thing.'

But Wood found that it was necessary to add new scenes to the film to make it comprehensible to a mass audience, and Frederic Raphael, who had scripted *Darling* and *Far from the Madding Crowd*, was drafted in to write them. Wood explained:

At that time, Hollywood insisted that everything should look plausible and real. Any elements of fantasy in them, unless they had music, like *The Wizard of Oz*, were

131

mistrusted. In rough cut, no one could understand what *In Search of Gregory* was about, so we had to do extra scenes. The brief I gave Frederic was along the lines of, 'Oh, Fred, can you make the audience understand this?' The subject itself got away. There's little you can do about that, because often you don't know what you've got, what the fish in the net is. I did a lot of Tom Stoppard plays on stage and wondered whether they were going to work, but they did.

Production on the picture finished in the autumn of 1968, but it was not released in Britain until November 1969. With an apparent waning of her appeal at the box office, Christie took a prolonged break from acting while waiting for better scripts to come along. She did, however, appear uncredited in crowd scenes for the Olympics film *The Games*—seen wearing outsize spectacles—during its shooting in Rome as a favour to director Michael Winner, who had seen her star potential back in 1963 but was told by a producer not to use her.

For Winner, staging the film's climactic marathon scenes through the streets of the Italian capital and ending up in the Olympic stadium was a mammoth task. Eleven cameras were scattered throughout Rome to give the impression of a continuous event and the director had to whittle the resulting seventeen hours of film down to fifteen minutes. Unfortunately, *The Games* did not attract audiences to the cinema and the American trade paper *Variety* listed it among Twentieth Century-Fox's top ten box-office disasters, with a $2 million loss. During that visit to Rome, Christie also dropped in on Dirk Bogarde, her *Darling* co-star, who had just started renting a house there.

As the 1960s came to a close, there was the real danger that Christie's career had already passed its best, with only a handful of stand-out films to her credit. Britain's brightest new screen actress, as she was in the middle of the decade, might be displaced by other newcomers, who included Judy Geeson and Jacqueline Bisset. Others, too, had achieved stardom in the intervening years, such as Vanessa Redgrave, another protégée of the Frinton Summer Theatre, and Susannah York, who was enjoying a comeback. While looking for that elusive script, Christie enjoyed her new-found love with American actor Warren Beatty.

CHAPTER TEN

WARREN BEATTY—LOVER AND GO-BETWEEN

Christie and legendary Hollywood lover Warren Beatty provided the press and public with a long-running 'will they, won't they marry' saga. She became the actor's latest in a string of actress girlfriends, and long after the filming of *Petulia* was completed in San Francisco Beatty was reported to have been a frequent visitor to Christie there from Hollywood.

However, there is some doubt about whether their relationship had begun then. Director Richard Lester had 'no memory of him' in San Francisco, although admitted that he was 'not a very sociable person' during filming. Director of photography Nicolas Roeg had no recollection of seeing Beatty with Christie, but said, 'I remember Warren Beatty arriving with his lawyer, Jack Schwartzman, who was a friend of mine and went on to become a producer.'

Christie had certainly not broken off her engagement to Don Bessant at that stage. In fact, he visited her in the United States and the couple went to a rodeo near Lake Tahoe. In December 1967, Bessant's father, Eric, died suddenly of a heart attack at the age of fifty-six and Christie attended the funeral. 'So that the press wouldn't be around, she came in our car,' recalled Iris Bessant, Eric's sister-in-law. 'I don't think the split had anything to do with Warren Beatty,' said Bessant's mother, Betty. 'It was the fact that her career took her to America and it became increasingly difficult to keep the thing going. She was becoming very famous. It did make things a little difficult and Don wasn't into that kind of life. I think she had been over there a little while before Warren Beatty came about.'

Christie and Bessant had previously moved into a house in Selwood Terrace, off the Fulham Road, in south-west London, with the art teacher supervising decorating and new furnishings. Whether spending more time in the United States distanced the couple or whether Beatty simply wooed and won the British actress, Bessant disappeared quietly from Christie's life and she found herself in a much more high-profile relationship.

Beatty, younger brother of actress Shirley MacLaine, was renowned more as a playboy than an actor, having already romanced Joan Collins and Natalie Wood, before starting a relationship with French-born actress Leslie Caron, six years his senior. Beatty and Caron flitted between his Beverly Hills home and her five-storey Georgian townhouse overlooking Montpelier Square in Kensington, west

London, where the actress lived with the two children from her second marriage, to theatre director Peter Hall.

Beatty had met Caron in early 1963, shortly after she was nominated for an Oscar for her performance in *The L-Shaped Room*. Hall filed for divorce the following year, citing Beatty as co-respondent. The divorce was finalized in 1965 and Caron kept custody of their children on condition that they did not leave Britain. This meant that Beatty subsequently spent much of his time in London and made two particularly bad films there—*Promise Her Anything* and *Kaleidoscope*.

However, the experience of being in 'swinging' London, which was leading the world with its films, music and fashion, rubbed off on Beatty and would later enable him to bring a different attitude to Hollywood pictures. While in the British capital, he also met Christie. Whether or not he visited the actress on the set of *Petulia*, Beatty subsequently followed her to mainland Europe when she shot *In Search of Gregory* and spent time with her in Britain while she filmed *The Go-Between*. She travelled to Paris when he made *The Only Game in Town*, alongside Elizabeth Taylor, before the couple teamed up to make *McCabe & Mrs Miller* in Canada. This was similar to Beatty's previous routine with Caron. She was with him while making *Mickey One* in Chicago and he travelled to Jamaica

136

when she was filming *Father Goose* alongside Cary Grant.

Beatty and his new partner had much in common. They both shunned publicity— Christie feeling that she had been over-interviewed during the filming of *Doctor Zhivago*—and neither was willing to conform to the conventions of Hollywood, sometimes turning down scripts for what appeared to be certain blockbusters.

When Christie came into his life, Beatty was enjoying huge success with his first film as a producer, *Bonnie and Clyde*, in which he and newcomer Faye Dunaway starred as the violent, young 1930s bankrobbers. Ironically, the origins of that picture went back to director François Truffaut, who turned down the chance to make it because he was planning his production of *Fahrenheit 451*, starring Christie.

At the time, Beatty was desperately searching for a film to produce—and possibly one in which he could star with Leslie Caron after the disappointment of *Promise Her Anything*—to take his career on to a higher plane. Caron knew Truffaut and arranged lunch with him on a trip to Paris; Beatty joined them for coffee. The actor showed interest in *Fahrenheit 451*, but the director said he had already cast the two lead roles.

However, Truffaut explained that two young American writers, David Newman and Robert

Benton, had sent him a script about outlaws Bonnie Parker and Clyde Barrow, who had been killed by Texas Rangers in 1934 after mounting a reign of terror in Texas and Oklahoma. These New York writers did not believe that Hollywood could put across the story without sensationalizing it and turning it into a Western, so they had approached Truffaut, who helped them to develop it.

As a result of the Paris meeting, Beatty bought the rights to the script, made the film, rejected Caron for the role of Bonnie and, after mixed reviews on its release in America in August 1967, managed to persuade distributors Warner to reopen it at bigger cinemas. The audiences came in their droves and some critics who abhorred the picture's violence were encouraged to reassess their original judgements. In the end, the film took more than $30 million at the box office in its first year.

When *Bonnie and Clyde* was nominated for ten Oscars, Christie accompanied Beatty to the awards ceremony in April 1968. In the event, the film won only two Academy Awards—Best Supporting Actress for Estelle Parsons and Best Cinematography for Burnett Guffey—but Beatty's failure to land the big ones of Best Picture and Best Actor were compensated for by the new love in his life. Christie stayed on in the United States afterwards, living with Beatty in the ninth-floor penthouse suite at the Beverly Wilshire hotel, in Beverly Hills, which he had already been renting. It comprised two rooms, a bathroom and a private terrace, where, with little to do in the suburban area around the hotel, they spent much of their time.

Then Beatty travelled with Christie to Geneva for the filming of *In Search of Gregory*, after which they decamped to Paris, where Beatty made *The Only Game in Town* with Elizabeth Taylor. Although set in Las Vegas, the film, based on a failed Broadway play, was made in the French capital so that Taylor could be close to husband Richard Burton, who was there making *Staircase*.

Filming finished in early 1969, with a few days' location shooting in Los Angeles, but the picture—like *In Search of Gregory*—was not released until the following year and was a total disaster. Beatty and Christie took a break from acting, both desperate not to take on anything else that might signal their fall down the ladder of success.

All the globetrotting had been interrupted only for Beatty's political commitments in the run-up to the 1968 presidential election, when he campaigned for the Democratic Party. It was a momentous time in American politics, with the party's candidate, Robert Kennedy, being assassinated on the day that he won the California primary, almost five years after the same fate had befallen his brother John as president.

Beatty's contribution to the Democratic campaign went beyond a star giving vocal support to the party. He read all of Kennedy's speeches made as a senator and took an active part in the campaign. After Kennedy's death, Beatty gave support to Senator George McGovern, but Hubert Humphrey emerged as the election contender's replacement. When election day came, he was defeated by Republican candidate Richard Nixon, but the experience of taking part in a political campaign, and his contribution to the Democrats in subsequent campaigns, gave Beatty material for later films such as *Shampoo* and *Bulworth*.

It also provided Christie with her first insight into party politics. On 6 July 1968, just a month after Kennedy's assassination, she accompanied Beatty to an American baseball game at Candlestick Park, San Francisco, where he addressed the crowd on the need for firearms restrictions before a match between the San Francisco Giants and the St Louis Cardinals. The crowd booed him, with the screen violence of *Bonnie and Clyde* fresh in their minds. That evening, the couple made for Cow Palace stadium, where Beatty made a similar speech before the heavyweight boxing match between Sonny Liston and Henry Clark. There, too, he had to fend off questions about on- and off-screen violence, as well as an onslaught of bottles and beer cans.

This introduction to politics triggered Christie's participation in demonstrations against America's involvement in the Vietnam War, including that outside the US Embassy in Grosvenor Square, London, in November 1969. More than 2,000 demonstrators had marched peacefully through the capital city before a group burned the Stars and Stripes outside the embassy and police stopped all the marchers getting close to the building.

Beatty's involvement with Christie meant that he was often in London, where he became good friends with film director Roman Polanski and his actress wife, Sharon Tate. The foursome sometimes dined with Playboy organization executive Victor Lownes at the Playboy Club. It was a shock in August 1969 when, after the pregnant Tate's return to Los Angeles, news came of her murder and that of four others there. Beatty was one of those close friends who flew to the United States with Polanski, who had been delayed from returning with his wife because of work commitments.

Christie kept her life with Beatty, in London and the United States, totally under wraps, revealing little even to friends. 'It was a very private world,' said one friend, 'We never knew much about her lifestyle because she was so secretive. As far as we could tell, when she wasn't travelling with Warren she spent her time making little glass ornaments and figurines which she carefully wrapped and sent to her friends. You would see them everywhere.'

It was Beatty who was enlisted to persuade Christie finally to return to the screen, in director Joseph Losey's classy version of L.P. Hartley's Edwardian novel *The Go-Between*. She was to star alongside Alan Bates, one of her suitors in *Far from the Madding Crowd*.

Losey had endured a seven-year struggle to film the story, about a boy, Leo Colston, who stays at a schoolfriend's stately home one hot summer at the beginning of the twentieth century and witnesses the *mores* of the English upper classes. He acts as a messenger for handsome tenant farmer Ted Burgess and his friend's beautiful elder sister, Marian, who are conducting a passionate affair while she is engaged to be married to wounded Boer War veteran Viscount Trimingham. Leo develops a crush on Marian and admires Ted.

At a party organized for his thirteenth birthday, the affair is discovered and Leo's collusion unmasked. Marian's hysterical mother drags the boy through the rain to an outbuilding where the couple are discovered making love together in a hayloft. Ted shoots himself and a pregnant Marian marries Trimingham, who accepts the child as his own. When Trimingham dies young, Marian is left with only her memories. More than fifty years later, in old age, Leo returns to the hall to exorcize the demons that have left him with an incapacity for love and a lifetime of bachelorhood, in flash-forward scenes that are intercut throughout the film.

Losey's picture captured the atmosphere of the society in which this tragedy took place, with scenes of croquet, cricket matches and picnics, large rooms and echoing corridors, elegant costumes, and photography that reflected the essence of the English countryside in summers long ago.

American-born Losey, who was forced into exile by the McCarthy witch-hunt against those alleged to have Communist sympathies, had suggested the idea of adapting the 1950s novel—based on writer Hartley's own experience in the summer of 1911—to writer Harold Pinter as far back as 1963. They had just made *The Servant*, the first of their three celebrated film collaborations, but Pinter pronounced himself wary of tampering with what he saw as a perfectly crafted novel.

Director Alexander Korda had originally bought the rights to make a screen version of *The Go-Between*, seeing it as a vehicle for Alec Guinness, but these passed on to Robert Velaise, with addresses in Liechtenstein and London. In 1964 Losey abandoned the idea of making the film, even though Pinter had eventually acceded to writing a first draft of the screenplay. Three years later, a court case involving Velaise and Hartley resulted in a compromise that would allow the rights owner to be nominal executive producer of any film adaptation, and in 1968 Pinter began work on a second draft.

Meanwhile, Losey travelled around Norfolk looking for suitable locations. West Bradenham Hall, the real-life setting for Hartley's novel, set in 1911, had changed so much in the intervening years that Losey dismissed it for his purposes. After seeing almost thirty houses, he eventually found an ideal location at Melton Hall, in the beautiful village of Melton Constable, between Norwich and Norfolk's north coast, although the lack of a double staircase and a garden meant the need for some use of a location at Blickling, about eight miles away.

L.P Hartley took a close interest in the production planning after the court case paved the way for a film. At first, when Losey was searching for an unknown actress to play Marian in her late teens, Hartley suggested one who was married to his godson. In a meeting with Bernard Delfont, chairman and chief executive of the Associated British Picture Corporation, which was providing the financial backing, Losey came up with a number of names but met with a negative response to each one. Mia Farrow, star of the film *Rosemary's Baby* and Losey's 1968 picture *Secret Ceremony*, had been approached by him, but she gave birth to twins in January 1970 and could not be persuaded to take the role.

Even before that, Losey consulted the agent of Lynn Redgrave, who had starred in the bawdy romp *Tom Jones* and the 'swinging London' film *Georgy Girl*. Among other names listed by Losey as possible candidates for the role of Marian were Christie; Marianne Faithfull, the pop singer-turned-actress who starred in *Girl on a Motorcycle* and was girlfriend of Rolling Stone Mick Jagger; Jane Asher, a former child star who then had only a handful of pictures behind her as an adult; Judi Bowker, soon to become known as doctor's daughter Vicky in *The Adventures of Black Beauty* on television; Sarah Miles, who had been thought of by David Lean to play Lara in *Doctor Zhivago*; Vivien Heilbron, subsequently to act Catriona in the 1971 film version of *Kidnapped*; Nicola Pagett, about to make her name as Elizabeth Bellamy in the television series *Upstairs, Downstairs*; Charlotte Rampling, the other female star of *Georgy Girl*; Prunella Ransome, another Joseph Janni—John Schlesinger discovery, who appeared alongside Christie in *Far from the Madding Crowd*; and Anjelica Huston, the American actress then still in her teens.

Then Losey, Pinter and John Heyman, the executive producer, thrashed out a solution during a meeting in a pub. Heyman and Pinter were adamant that the heartless and selfish

Marian should be played by Christie, whom Losey had considered for the role back in 1964, when she would have been acceptable as an actress playing a part a few years younger—although even then she considered herself too old. This meant that Losey had a battle to convince her six years later that she should take the part. So he used a previous acquaintance with Beatty—who had been set to star for him in an unmade espionage thriller, *The Most Dangerous Game*—to persuade Christie. Still waiting to hear her verdict, Losey cabled Beatty on 21 May 1970 that he 'would appreciate your giving definite answer today to John Heyman as the project otherwise has no more than a day's life in it'. Finally Christie committed herself to the film. Three weeks later, Losey cabled her to pronounce himself 'delighted we are finally going to work together'.

At a meeting urgently convened in the Dorchester Hotel, Losey had asked director of photography Gerry Fisher, who did much to give the film its nostalgic look, how he could make Christie look the age of the novel's heroine throughout the picture. Fisher recalled:

The subject of the meeting was the script as written, which called for a girl of about 18. Being truthful to that, Joe thought he should get a girl of 18, but he had difficulty finding finance because it was considered an arty picture without great financial prospects. The backers said, 'Can't you give us a star and can you make her look 18?'

So I was asked, could I make Julie Christie look 18? My response was, 'If you give me carte blanche so that each shot of her is entirely controlled to that purpose, it's conceivable. She could pass as 18 provided she could *play* 18. But, if you think I can make Julie Christie appear 18 and others look the age they are, with her taking tea round to people sitting at tables on the lawn on a summer's day, then no.

Losey considered this and still wondered whether he could find an actress of the right age, but pressure was on from the backers to feature major stars. Fisher explained:

Joe, ideally, would have preferred to make the picture with an 18-year-old girl. The finance people, apparently, were looking for a couple with box-office appeal. At that time, that meant the couple from *Far from the Madding Crowd*. Joe was told, 'If you get Julie Christie and Alan Bates, you will get the money.' That made a subtle change in the whole treatment, but the film works perfectly well—the boy is enamoured of a mature young woman. Within the situation of the story and creating another, more graceful age, one could somehow successfully overcome those hurdles because that was the style of the period—a lady was a lady. There was no mention of her age at all in the film.

Although Alan Bates eventually landed the role of Ted, others considered included Albert Finney, Tom Courtenay, David Warner, Michael Crawford, Mick Jagger, Malcolm McDowell, James Villiers, John McEnery, Peter McEnery, Ian McShane and John Stride. Leo was played by fourteen-year-old Dominic Guard. Others considered for that role included Nigel Havers and Peter Duncan, both of whom went on to find success, mainly on television. Also starring alongside Christie and Bates were Edward Fox as the scarred Viscount Trimingham; Margaret Leighton as Mrs Maudsley (after Deborah Kerr had turned down the role of Christie's neurotic mother); Michael Gough as the dominating Mr Maudsley; and Michael Redgrave playing the present-day Leo looking back at the events of his memorable summer in Norfolk. Throughout all the pre-production work, finding enough money to finance the film had been a problem for Losey. He shelved it in the spring of 1969 after the Associated British Picture Corporation was unable to provide all the budget. Bryan Forbes, the actor-director who had just become head of production at

Elstree Studios after EMI bought a controlling interest in ABPC, explained later, 'The projected budget proved an obstacle—some £680,000 as I recall—and much too rich for me to tackle alone.'

The following year, ABPC renewed its interest, only to back out again in April 1970, just three months before shooting was due to begin. To get the film back on track, Losey agreed to take a lower fee, with the gamble of accepting a percentage of profits to come. He persuaded most of the actors to do the same, although Christie was guaranteed $50,000, as well as equally sharing with Losey and Bates 10 per cent of EMI's gross receipts above production costs. By the time shooting was over, EMI had brought in MGM to co-finance the film.

Location filming began in Norfolk in July 1970, with Melton Hall becoming Brandham Hall, the reincarnation of the novel's West Bradenham Hall, and Christie found herself being publicly humiliated by Losey after arriving late on the set. 'I would accept that from a star like Elizabeth Taylor, but not from you,' he roared. Director of photography Gerry Fisher recalled, 'It's quite possible he said it to achieve a certain effect. Joe was nervous, too, and against anything that exhibited a disrespect to the pressure that we were under to realize the film.'

Everything combined successfully to

recreate that period, but the long, hot summer featured in Hartley's book did not start that way in Norfolk during filming, with little sun during the first two weeks. This meant constant schedule changes. 'We were all under the pressure of trying to maintain the serenity of this graceful period when we were up against extremely bad weather,' said Fisher. 'After preparing for one scene, we sometimes had to change to another. We might be ready for one outside, the weather would turn bad and Joe switched to another one inside, which would mean Julie changing into a different costume. Joe and Julie had a lot of talks together between scenes. She was entirely relaxed about her role.'

However, there was a dramatic improvement in the weather and working on the film proved a happy experience for many of those involved—including Roger Lloyd Pack, who acted the Maudsley family's houseguest, Charles. Referring to the pending birth of his daughter, who, as Emily Lloyd, became a film star in her own right, he said:

I remember a gorgeous summer, but I was very involved with my own private life because my wife was pregnant. I recall Julie lying in a hammock and Warren Beatty being around—he came on set at least once. It was the end of the Sixties and I had a feeling that Julie found it a burden being an icon, as she was. She was a bit of a free spirit and I'm sure she would rather have hung out with some of her mates and not have had to carry that responsibility.

I stayed on after the shoot and found a place on the estate where we filmed, which I still have. Julie lived in a cottage near Aylsham and stayed on for a while afterwards, too. Everyone fell in love with the place. It was a very happy shoot, in a lovely location, with lovely weather. *The Go-Between* was one of those rather dreamy films that don't come along often enough.

During shooting, which took little more than two months, Beatty joined Christie in a small, secluded cottage near the sea and she used a bicycle to travel around on. The press converged on Norfolk, viewing the couple as the new Richard Burton and Elizabeth Taylor. 'They all want to talk to Julie about her romance and Julie doesn't want to talk about that,' said Alan Bates at the time. 'Why should she?'

The actress was spending a prolonged period in the countryside for the first time since making *Far from the Madding Crowd*, and one significant event for Christie while making *The Go-Between* was her conversion to vegetarianism, after seeing pigs being slaughtered at a farm used for location shooting. 'It was so appalling,' she said. 'I just couldn't believe that that was what was meant by factory farming. Animals were being kept in a kind of concentration camp. I was a vegetarian from then on.' Beatty pledged his support and vowed he would never eat meat again. A decade later, Christie would give her support to animal rights on and off screen.

The film itself experienced even more battles before it came to the screen. Losey was unhappy with the score by distinguished composer Richard Rodney Bennett—who had worked on three of the director's previous films, as well as two of Christie's pictures, *Billy Liar!* and *Far from the Madding Crowd*—and brought in Michel Legrand to write something less dramatic. Losey wanted something melodic but unsentimental, although he acknowledged that his brief for Legrand was different from that for the original composer.

Then MGM decided to sell its American distribution rights to Columbia, after Losey and Bryan Forbes had insisted that the film be premiered at the Cannes Film Festival in May 1971, not in Beverly Hills. Shortly after MGM's action, Forbes resigned as EMI's head of production. John Heyman, one of the film's two producers, tried to persuade Losey and Pinter to cut out the picture's flash-forward sequences from 1900—in which the film was re-set—to the present day, which he found confusing. Rightly or wrongly, they firmly refused, although both Christie and director of photography Gerry Fisher believed that the scene featuring an elderly Leo returning to the house and sitting down with the widowed Marian—heavily made up and shot close-up in shadow—did not work. Fisher explained:

> The make-up was not good enough. Difficult as it would be to make somebody who's thirty look eighteen, which is only twelve years' difference, to make someone of thirty look seventy or eighty is even harder. I wasn't happy with her look—it looked like applied make-up. That's why I filmed it in shadow. But I'm very proud of the film. In many ways, it reflected my own childhood. In the long, hot summers, out of school, I would go to the fields and lie flat on my back in the corn and hear field mice and birds, and get the heat near the ground. I was very aware of that and tried to bring some of that feeling to the photography.

The picture received its Cannes premiere and won the writer and director the top prize of the Palme D'Or in the festival's Grand Prix for best film. It beat *Death in Venice*, made by Losey's long-time rival, Italian Luchino Visconti, and featuring Dirk Bogarde, who had starred in Losey and Pinter's two previous pictures together.

Christie did not attend the festival but arrived with Beatty for the New York premiere, at the 68th Street Playhouse, two months later. This provided another opportunity for the press to picture the couple together, although Christie had refused to do any publicity for *The Go-Between*, rather perplexing the film's producers and backers. Losey, meanwhile, threw himself into a merry-go-round of media interviews in New York. American critics gave the picture rave reviews and British writers did the same when it was released in the country of its production in September 1971—'a near-perfect example of adaptation,' David Robinson exclaimed in the *Financial Times*.

Although Britain's Society of Film and Television Arts (BAFTA's predecessor) presented awards to Pinter for Best Screenplay, Margaret Leighton as Best Supporting Actress, Edward Fox as Best Supporting Actor and Dominic Guard as Most Promising Newcomer, Christie and Bates won nothing. Leighton also received the film's only Oscar nomination. However, *The Go-Between* proved to be a good choice for Christie after her self-imposed exile. It won critical and public acclaim, earning more than $3 million from cinema and television screenings—although, to Losey and Pinter's annoyance, Columbia cut four seconds of Christie and Bates's hayloft sex scene for screening on American airlines and television stations.

CHAPTER ELEVEN

McCABE & MRS MILLER

By the time *The Go-Between* was released in the United States, Christie's next film was already playing in cinemas there, and it provided the critics and public with the spectacle of her first screen role alongside Warren Beatty. It also earned her a second Oscar nomination as Best Actress and the chance to work in Canada with another of the film world's top directors, Robert Altman, who had just made the Oscar-winning *M*A*S*H*.

In *McCabe & Mrs Miller*, Christie acted English cockney madam Constance Miller, who arrives in the small mining town of Presbyterian Church in America's Old West and runs a brothel. The operation is financed by cocky but gullible gambler John Q. McCabe, played by Beatty in fur coat with a bushy beard and flowing, dark hair. Based on Edmund Naughton's novel *McCabe*, a literary Western, the American-backed film was set at about the same time as *The Go-Between*, but its story and characters could not have been further removed from the gentility of Christie's previous picture.

Using money gained from winning poker games with zinc miners, McCabe has brought the ailing north-west town back to life by opening a saloon-bordello, buying three 'chippies' (prostitutes) for $200 and putting Mrs Miller in charge on her arrival from Britain. When he shares the madam's bed, she retains her pride by charging him. Mining speculators then try to buy out McCabe, and, when he refuses, send in gunmen, resulting in a bloody end for him and the townsfolk in the snow, as the small wooden church burns and Mrs Miller sinks into oblivion after finding solace in opium.

In fact, Christie had been signed up to star in *McCabe & Mrs Miller* prior to Beatty, and Elliott Gould had previously been considered to play McCabe. However, Beatty was considered a better box-office draw and came in as *ex officio* producer. Like *The Go-Between*, the film had taken a while to come to the screen. Rights had changed hands and by 1970 were controlled by producer David Foster, who had entered the film industry as an independent two years earlier after switching from a career in public relations. After speaking to Robert Altman's agent, George Litto, who packaged film and television productions, he was put in touch with the director, and Brian McKay wrote the screenplay in five weeks.

By the time location filming was due to start in the hills around Vancouver in October 1970, Altman had fallen out with McKay, his friend of ten years. As a result, he made changes to the script, now under the working title of *The Presbyterian Church Wager*, and allowed Beatty to adapt the character of McCabe to his own vision and Christie to rewrite her dialogue. Many people contributed to the script rewrites throughout the film, although it was officially credited to Altman and McKay.

'He [Altman] simply turned Julie's stuff over to her,' explained script supervisor Joan Tewkesbury. 'She had a companion with her who knew all the different kinds of dialects, and they would go off and take these scenes and redo them as a woman would do them in this position. And Warren would do the same thing. It was really wonderful to watch. They wrote very specifically because they needed lines, they needed script.'

Shooting went on into 1971, amid wind, rain and snow. Christie and Beatty shared a small cottage with friends at Horseshoe Bay, on Howe Sound, hiding themselves in seclusion as they had previously done in Norfolk.

At this time, speculation about whether the couple were planning to marry—or had even done so in secret—was at its height. Asked whether they were married, Christie would say only, 'If we are, we are, if we're not, we're not.' Her mother, Rosemary, and agent, Michael Linnit, both gave similarly frustrating replies to enquiring journalists. All this proved was that the enigmatic couple would not deign to give the press or public any information about their private life together. One morsel of information that did come out during filming was that Christie was suffering an eye ailment.

On the set, Altman—an American director who defied many of the film-making conventions of Hollywood—was making what was to become one of his finest films, an anti-Western depicting the squalid realities of frontier life rather than reinforcing the myths created in the pictures of John Wayne and Randolph Scott.

The realism of a town being built was achieved through doing simply that as filming went along; the burning of the church was intended to show people trying to save a building that they never used but that was respected because of its symbolism. To build from scratch production designer Leon Ericksen's frontier town, with two saloons, whorehouse and bath-house, cabins, barber shop, sawmill, general store and steepled church, was a remarkable achievement.

Altman was generous in his praise of Christie and the depth she brought to the part of the cockney madam, doing many of her scenes in one take. Altman liked to shoot that way, although this was at variance with Beatty's method of working up to his best performance. In scenes with Beatty, Christie would perform 'each take over and over again, the same, only richer, each time', explained

Joan Tewkesbury.

Christie was particularly effective in times of silence, at one moment revealing her escape from pain and loneliness by tracing with her finger the words in a book, glimpsed through a window with lamplight on her curly hair—in fact, a wig.

The whole look of the film, created by director of photography Vilmos Zsigmond, was of muted colours, with the saloon covered by a diffuse green haze and the brothel bathed in a red-orange glow. Scenes involving both Christie and Beatty were often lit to show them in amber. All of this gave McCabe & Mrs Miller an evocative feel. 'We preflashed every foot of film,' said Altman, 'and when you do that you pick up grain, plus the fact that we used fog filters with it and it desaturates the colour.'

Altman's style of using overlapping dialogue and lines that trail off suited Christie perfectly, although the muffled sound was seized on by some critics. This was largely the result of the bad weather, and Altman disliked dubbing. Montreal-born folk singer Leonard Cohen's wistful songs, although also criticized by some at the time, were another ingredient that helped to capture the atmosphere of *McCabe & Mrs Miller*.

On its release, the film was generally well received, with some reservations. One reviewer, pointing out that Christie was twenty pounds lighter than she was in *Petulia*, her previous American film, ventured that 'to compare her whore-with-a-heart-of-gold with Jane Fonda's in *Klute* is a lesson in the animation of stereotypes' and noted that 'the whores, for once, look like whores and not like the Goldwyn Girls, and the miners are a group of people rather than a string of extras'. For Christie, taking a role that extended her range proved to be a good decision and she was nominated for a Best Actress Oscar once more, although she lost out to Jane Fonda for her performance as a call-girl in *Klute*.

After finishing *McCabe & Mrs Miller*, Christie took another long break before returning to the cinema, happy simply to savour her time with Beatty. Continuing to be discerning about her scripts, she turned down a reported $400,000 to take the title role in a remake of the Greta Garbo picture *Camille*, meanwhile displaying a Garbo-style reticence by shunning the press and public. Nothing, moreover, came of plans for Christie to star in Swedish actress-director Mal Zetterling's planned screen version of *Bury Me in My Boots*, which was based on Sally Trent's autobiography about her experience of leaving a comfortable suburban home to share the life of London's tramps. In the event, the film was not made.

Beatty himself had previously turned down *Butch Cassidy and the Sundance Kid*, and over the next couple of years rejected *The Sting*, *The Way We Were* and *The Great Gatsby*, all four of which became classics starring Robert Redford. He also shied away from the role that Marlon Brando eventually played in *Last Tango in Paris*.

While in Hamburg making the totally forgettable *$* (retitled *The Heist* in Britain), in which he played a security expert who steals safe deposit boxes, Beatty was almost killed after falling on a railway line in front of a goods train. He pulled himself out of its path only at the last moment and was lucky to suffer just a torn ligament in one ankle. In a nearby hospital, on answering questions from a German clerk filling in admission forms, Beatty was asked whether he was married. 'No, but I'm in love!' he replied.

Beatty had bought himself a secluded house in Mulholland Drive, on a high mountain road overlooking Los Angeles and connecting several canyons, but he and Christie never lived in it, preferring to stay at the Beverly Wilshire hotel. Beatty was out on the political campaign trail again when he supported Democratic candidate George McGovern's bid to unseat Richard Nixon as president in the 1972 election—and Christie was at his side. Nixon won by a landslide, but Beatty had put a huge amount of effort into the campaign as national vice-chairman of McGovern's fund-raising committee and was credited with

161

inventing the 'political concert', with major stars giving their time to boost party funds in cities across the United States. Directing the stage shows himself, he even persuaded Carole King to come out of temporary retirement to perform in Los Angeles and enticed Peter, Paul and Mary and Simon and Garfunkel to reunite at Madison Square Garden, New York.

However, by late 1972, when Christie left to make her next film, the supernatural chiller *'Don't Look Now'*, in England and Venice, her romance with Beatty appeared to be over and he was soon escorting other women. Nevertheless, Christie returned to the United States in the spring of 1973 and watched him in Washington State on the set of his political thriller *The Parallax View*, in which he played a reporter investigating a senator's assassination. When she acted on the Broadway stage in *Uncle Vanya*, Christie continued to see him there, flying the 3,000-mile trip each weekend.

She has always refused to comment on her relationship with Beatty, but his womanizing ways could not have helped matters. In 1970, while Christie was finishing work on *The Go-Between*, actress Britt Ekland fell for him in London. They made love in her bedsitter and she subsequently stayed at the Beverly Wilshire with Beatty when she visited Los Angeles to appear on Dean Martin's television show. The affair ended after two months, when Ekland had to return to London to discuss a television play.

'Warren was the most divine lover of all,' Ekland wrote in her autobiography. 'His libido was as lethal as high octane gas. I had never known such pleasure and passion in my life. Warren could handle women as smoothly as operating an elevator. He knew exactly where to locate the top button. One flick and we were on the way.' But Ekland was always aware of Beatty's relationship with Christie, who was 'foolishly absent, and loyalty wasn't his strongest point'. She added, 'Warren was always apprehensive about our affair, just in case Julie found out.'

Joan Collins, one of Beatty's previous lovers, reported similarly that his 'main passion' was 'making love—and he was also able to accept phone calls at the same time. I had heard that men were at their sexual peak between the ages of seventeen and twenty-three. If Warren was anything to go by, this was true. I had never known anyone like him before.'

A hint that Christie made the decision to drop Beatty came when he later commented, 'The truth is that whenever a relationship has ended the decision has never been mine; it's always been the other person's.'

Two years after breaking up with Christie, Beatty began another long-term relationship, with Michelle Phillips, who as Michelle Gilliam had been a member of the legendary

American singing group the Mamas and the Papas, enjoying hits such as 'California Dreamin' and 'Monday, Monday', and she later found success as an actress. After divorcing Mamas and Papas singer John Phillips, she had in 1970 been married to actor Dennis Hopper for eight days and, before falling for Beatty, had lived with Jack Nicholson.

This time Beatty and his partner—plus her daughter, China—did move into the Mulholland Drive house, with its swimming pool, lagoon, Jacuzzi and tennis court. However, Beatty kept on his penthouse suite and Phillips rented her own apartment. Despite the split, Christie continued to hold Beatty in high regard and was to make two more films with him.

CHAPTER TWELVE

'DON'T LOOK . . .'

Christie proved her ability to choose roles out of the mainstream and project them in a totally 'unstarry' way, in the macabre supernatural thriller *Don't Look Now*. She played Laura Baxter, who with husband John tries to come to terms with the death of her young daughter. The eerie elements of the film, shot mostly in wintertime Venice, were enhanced by a legendary sex scene between Christie and co-star Donald Sutherland. Considered so explicit at the time that censors in America insisted on a minor cut to it, the scene was allowed to remain intact in Britain, where it was regarded as tasteful and essential to the story. One of Christie's finest pictures, *'Don't Look Now'* achieved cult status and is remembered as a cinematic masterpiece.

The film, a British-Italian co-production, was the third that Nicolas Roeg had made as director, following the distinctive *Walkabout* and *Performance*, and it gained him recognition as one of Britain's best new film-makers, with a talent for using images to show the natural and supernatural existing alongside each other. He had previously won acclaim as a director of photography and worked with Christie on *Fahrenheit 451*, *Far from the Madding Crowd* and *Petulia*. And he had started in that capacity on *Doctor Zhivago* before differences of opinion with director David Lean led to his sacking.

'Don't Look Now' started as a screen version of a short story by Daphne du Maurier, with a script by Allan Scott and Chris Bryant. 'We were hired by a producer, Peter Katz, to write the screenplay,' recalled Scott. 'There was a lot of material original to the screenplay and we worked on it with an American director, Larry Peerce. He left the project and it went to Nic

Roeg. We developed the script further with him.'

Roeg was keen to feature a husband and wife who originated from different countries, and from the start considered that Christie and Canadian actor Donald Sutherland were a good match. The director explained:

I rather like the idea of nationally mixed marriages—they are the only real *entente cordiale*, an alliance founded on the battleground of love, the bed. I thought Julie was tremendous and I had enjoyed working with her before. I had never seen anyone else in it but was told that she was in America, working on the McGovern presidential campaign. Also, Donald was involved with another movie, so they were both unavailable. The American producer then talked about casting Robert Wagner and Natalie Wood. I think they were approached, but I didn't get Julie and Donald out of my mind. At the same time, the movie schedule was put back several times. I never heard much more about Robert and Natalie—maybe their agents thought the movie had fallen through. But what did fall through was the McGovern campaign, and George McGovern not getting the Democratic Party candidacy was pretty startling. I realized that Julie would be free and, oddly enough, the film that

166

Donald was working on collapsed, so he was free, too. I felt they had come to the film—it belonged to them.

'I haven't a clue why Nic wanted me,' said Christie. 'All I knew was that I wanted to work with him. I was impressed by the script—it was unusual in the way it came at things tangentially . . . The whole film could have gone completely haywire, it was a bit of a risk, but I don't like run-of-the-mill stuff. In the event the risk paid off.'

The picture, costing $1.2 million, was a co-production between Casey Productions of London and Eldorado Films of Rome, and it became the first box-office success in years for British Lion, the distributor in Britain. In search of a new screen identity, Sutherland—who had co-starred with Jane Fonda in both of his two previous films, *Klute* and *Steelyard Blues*—found a completely different head of curly hair, courtesy of a Hollywood wig-maker.

Before shooting began, Roeg took Christie to a seance for research purposes, because a scene in the film involved her character taking part in one with two elderly spinster sisters who apparently have paranormal powers and claim to have seen her dead daughter. Direct voice medium Leslie Flint allowed the director and actress to attend a session of his that was being observed by some American parapsychologists. 'It was interesting and I would have liked to have attended more and really gone into it,' said Christie. 'But I didn't have the time. I went with an open mind— open to anything that might happen. I enjoyed it. I was quite scared when I thought I heard voices. But, then, I'm easily scared anyway!'

Roeg was intrigued by the presence of people at the seance with totally opposing views. He recalled:

There were some who wanted help in their grief, who were bringing a belief and hope with them, and others who were there looking for cold, hard, clinical proof. I went along hoping to be completely amazed and I was, because I found two completely different sets of people there for different reasons. It reflected very clearly what our lives are about, all doing things separately for our own agendas. In the film, John wanted to get Laura away from moving into obsession and dejection, he wanted them to move on. As intimate and loving a couple as they were, a mutual grief is sometimes too awful to bear.

Shooting of *'Don't Look Now'* started in Britain in December 1972 with a week on location in Hertfordshire, at the home of veteran film and stage comedy actor David Tree. He had lost an arm during service in the Second World War, but in his late fifties was persuaded to come out of retirement to play a schoolmaster. The large house and its grounds were used for the opening scene, in which the Baxters' daughter, Christine, dressed in a shiny red mackintosh, drowns in the garden pond after trying to recover a ball—an event foreseen by father John, a church restorer, as he looks at slides of stained-glass windows through a projector, then sees a red stain spread across one of them. It is apparent that John has powers of extra-sensory perception.

Difficulty in persuading Sharon Williams, the child actress who played Christine, to go underwater resulted in a neighbouring farmer's daughter taking over and practising the scene in which Sutherland pulls her out of the pond, but she backed out after being dressed in the mackintosh. So a 'double' was used and the critical moments were finally performed in a water tank, resulting in three different girls being filmed for that one sequence.

After a Christmas break, filming moved to Venice for the rest of the picture, with shooting taking place during January and February 1973 in an out-of-season, empty city, using a largely Italian crew. Locations included the Europa Hotel, where the Baxters were staying in the story, although interiors of their suite were shot at the Bauer Grunwald, which provided more room for the crew and equipment. After much searching for a setting for scenes in which John is seen working on the restoration of a Byzantine church, Roeg and his Italian location manager discovered an ideal, small church, Santo Nicolo dei Mendici, on the outskirts of the city, next to the water. It was even undergoing repair, with scaffolding around it and a poster proclaiming that the work was being paid for by Britain's Venice in Peril fund. Venice was deliberately portrayed not so much as a popular tourist resort as a maze of narrow streets and alleyways in which it was easy to get lost.

During the shoot, Christie stayed at a friend's villa in Giudecca, with huge wrought-iron gates at the bottom of the formal garden that opened to give a view of the water beyond. She enjoyed filming in the beautiful city and recalled a walk through the streets at night with Roeg and director of photography Tony Richmond, who had previously worked with Christie and Roeg as the camera focus-puller on *Fahrenheit 451* and *Far from the Madding Crowd.* 'We were half-cut,' she said, 'and wandered through all these mysterious, damp alleyways looking at the reflection of the water on the wet stone and the reflection of the buildings in the canals. I loved it.'

Filming was hampered only by the changing levels of tides, which caused continuity problems and difficulty in transporting equipment under bridges at high tide. The title of the film came from a line in the book, but not used in the film, in which John spots the psychic spinsters in a restaurant and tells Laura, 'Don't look now, but there are a couple of old girls two tables away who are trying to hypnotize me.'

The befriending of Laura by the sisters, when the blind one claims to have seen the dead girl sitting between her parents in the restaurant, causes friction between her and John. The couple are further distanced from one another after Laura kisses the ring on the finger of a Venetian bishop who has been a good friend to them, leaving John out in the cold as he treads his own escape route from grief.

The supernatural nature of *'Don't Look Now'* combines with the thriller element of the story, in which a serial killer is on the loose in Venice. Echoing the red mackintosh worn by the Baxters' daughter when she drowned, the murderer is revealed to be a female dwarf in a similar, hooded coat, and the funeral witnessed by John at one point in the film turns out to be his own—after dying at the hands of this figure. When the funeral happens for real, Laura smiles, knowing that her husband and daughter are now together, happy.

The hypnotic, four-minute sex sequence was constructed at the time of filming. 'It was almost entirely improvised,' explained Allan Scott. 'The script simply said, "They make love." That was because, at the time of writing the screenplay, Nic Roeg wasn't sure what he could ask the actors to do and what they felt comfortable doing.'

Performing the sequence did not come naturally to Christie. 'People didn't do scenes like that in those days,' she said. 'There were no available examples, no role models, and I did find it difficult. I just went blank and Nic shouted instructions. I hardly knew Donald then, either, but apart from being a bloody good actor he's a responsible one and took responsibility for the scene, helping me through it.' The action was shot with just Roeg and two technicians in the room.

The simulated love-making, sometimes in the most contorted of positions, was intercut with shots of Christie and Sutherland dressing for dinner afterwards in the bathroom and bedroom, a novel idea that helped to instil the sense of jumps forward in time that occurred throughout the film. Intensely erotic, the scene was also conceived as the portrayal of sex firmly rooted in a marriage, involving a couple who had been together for years and knew each other's bodies intimately, as well as portraying the togetherness they both craved at a time of great loss. Roeg explained:

The love scene is not a seduction. Making love in marriage is part of your life and I wanted to have a sense that, at that time, maybe they would try for another child. It wasn't a case of, 'Let's go out to dinner and, afterwards, come back and have a coffee with me.' There was no daring in it—it was love-making. They felt at ease, at home with each other. They are getting ready for dinner, she has a robe on, is reading a magazine on the bed and says to him, 'Look at this,' and he touches her. Sometimes a wave of emotion comes over you and you think, 'I love this woman. I like you a lot.' And then they make love.

I didn't want them to go through their whole gymnastic performance. I wanted to see the expressions on their faces, their heartfelt emotions, as well as showing them afterwards. After love-making with someone you do love and someone you don't love, it's a very different affair. Intercutting it like that also accelerates everything, instead of having a long scene where they make love, then they get out of bed and get dressed. It also leads people to think they're seeing more.

So I wanted it cut up and to see their satisfaction with each other after so many bad things had happened to them and the pressure they were under. I realized that most of the time they had been bickering, nagging at each other. After I finished the film, I cut it with the love scene both in and out. With it out, they *are* bickering all the time.

However, Allan Scott was remarkable in having his eyes on one of the props in the scene. 'At the time, I was chairman of a whisky company and Nic kindly agreed to put a bottle of whisky on the bedside table,' revealed Scott. 'So I was the only person never to see the love-making because I was more concerned with the product placement!'

For those with their eyes on the action, the sequence turned out to be a landmark in cinema, featuring major stars in as graphic a portrayal of sex as anyone was likely to have viewed since Marlon Brando spent most of *Last Tango in Paris* coupling with Maria Schneider. Christie had, of course, helped to make the portrayal of oral sex acceptable on screen when she took it in her stride, lying down, in *Darling*, but it was not until after the success of that film that she became a name to be reckoned with.

Before the release of *'Don't Look Now'*, newspapers seized on the sex scene and filled many column inches with the prospect of the film censors banning it and questioning how authentic the love-making was between Christie and Sutherland. 'They didn't *make love*,' insisted director Roeg a quarter of a century later, apparently weary of, and slightly bemused by, the idea that the action went beyond simulation.

At the time, the *Daily Mail* informed its readers, 'One of the frankest sex scenes ever to be filmed is likely to plunge lovely Julie Christie into the biggest censorship row since *Last Tango in Paris*. Her latest film is expected to push back even further the frontiers of screen permissiveness.' There was no row, but the American censor advised Roeg that 'humping' and 'the rise and fall between thighs' would not be tolerated. With new obscenity laws requiring American cinemas to make their own decisions on censorship, at the risk of being prosecuted, no one there was taking any risks. As a result, the director removed nine frames from the scene for screening there, although the picture was still given an 'R' (Restricted) certificate. The offending frames, showing Sutherland's pubic hair, constituted only one-third of a second's screen time. Stephen Murphy of the British Board of Film Censors passed *'Don't Look Now'* uncut, but insisted on giving it an X-certificate.

The picture received its premiere at the Odeon, Leicester Square, London, in October 1973 and was soon filling cinemas across the country. Critics, particularly those in the more serious newspapers and film magazines, warmed to it, one noting that Roeg found 'a whole new range of expressions in Julie Christie's face to illustrate Laura's strange duplicity'. American critics also gave *'Don't*

Look Now' favourable reviews when it was released there two months later, some even comparing it to *Rosemary's Baby*, director Roman Polanski's 1968 film about a woman's husband becoming involved in a witches' coven.

On the first television screening in Britain of *'Don't Look Now'*, in 1979, the BBC cut the sex scene, with the result that many viewers wrote in asking for it to be reinstated. So when it was shown again four years later no cuts were made. The film continued to be talked about and examined over subsequent decades, but, once the shooting was over, Christie made the decision to return to the stage, before making another Hollywood picture.

CHAPTER THIRTEEN

LAST DAYS IN HOLLYWOOD

It was not long before Christie was back in the United States, watching Warren Beatty filming *The Parallax View* and making her Broadway debut in *Uncle Vanya*. She had not acted on stage since 1964 and her role as Elena would be her last for more than twenty years. On travelling to New York in May 1973, Christie said she felt 'real terror' at acting alongside stars such as George C. Scott, Lillian Gish,

176

Cathleen Nesbitt and Barnard Hughes, and performing live in front of an audience, unlike in a film where 'if you fall flat on your face . . . you shoot the scene again'. Theatre was always Christie's least-preferred medium and she was given no encouragement to continue in it after reviews of her Broadway performance.

Celebrated director Mike Nichols, inspired to do the Chekhov play because his father was a Russian doctor, had persuaded Christie to take part. He wanted the play to revolve around Elena, an old professor's young wife. 'I had no intention of doing it,' she said. 'It seemed impossible. I would not have done it if it wasn't for Mike.' Before the production opened at the Circle in the Square—Joseph E. Levine Theatre, Nichols put the cast through five weeks of rehearsals, even trying to help them relax by doing one read-through in a rehearsal room while lying on beds moved from their dressing-rooms.

The production's entire eight-week run was a sell-out, but it received a mixed reception from critics. Christie fared even worse. In the *New York Times*, Walter Kerr panned the play and added, 'Miss Christie herself is bland in her often-announced ennui, unable to cope with a second-half soliloquy and burdened— late in the play—with a wig that makes her look as though she had walked through a meringue factory.' She fared no better in *Variety*, whose critic, 'Hobe', wrote, 'Her performance in the later scenes where the character opens out seems muted, and there is little suggestion of suppressed anguish as she rejects the doctor and departs for virtual exile with her fatuous old husband.'

The 'butchers of Broadway' were enough to keep Christie off the stage for another two decades, but she had no intention of leaving the United States. After buying a remote, derelict farmhouse in New Jersey, the announcement the next year that she was to star in another film with Beatty came as no surprise.

The sex comedy *Shampoo*, set against the backdrop of the 1968 American presidential election, featured Christie's sometime lover as a womanizing Beverly Hills hairdresser—a role that clearly reflected his own weakness for the opposite sex. Women and politics were the two main strands in his life outside his work, and Christie had been there with Beatty when he supported the Democrats in their 1968 campaign.

In fact, the idea for the film had come from Beatty and his friend, screenwriter Robert Towne, back in 1967 after the actor's success as a producer with *Bonnie and Clyde*. At that time, there were no political ingredients, but Towne's original script was put to one side and forgotten until 1974. By then Beatty had come up with his own script and, after getting together at the Beverly Wilshire hotel to thrash out a final version, the pair were jointly credited as writers, with Hal Ashby directing. Towne had just worked with Ashby on his previous film, *The Last Detail*, starring Jack Nicholson. Ashby himself had only three years earlier directed *Harold and Maude*, which became a cult black comedy.

Inevitably, interviewers and critics drew comparisons between Beatty and hairdresser George Roundy in *Shampoo*, who cheats on wife Jill by having affairs with older married woman Felicia, Felicia's daughter Lorna and Felicia's husband's mistress, Jackie, played by Christie. 'I'd like to suck his cock,' Jackie says in one of the film's most memorable lines, as she sits down at an election-night banquet with a group of people, including George's wife, played by Goldie Hawn. Jackie then disappears under the table to fulfil her wish.

Speculation refused to die about whether Christie and Beatty were still romantically involved, but he was reported to be dating other women, including Carrie Fisher, who played Lorna in *Shampoo*. By the time the film was released in the United States in February 1975, he had taken up with Michelle Phillips.

'My own personal life was probably distracting,' Beatty admitted more than twenty years later. 'I probably was having a little too much fun at that point in life and I always thought this central character, this hairdresser, was kind of pathetic. I felt he was a person who could hardly respond in these circumstances, was exhausted with what he felt were his obligations to the people that he encountered.' The actor added that in *Shampoo* he tried to equate personal promiscuity with political promiscuity, where politicians offered promises that were not carried out.

Other stars of the film, which was shot in sixty days, included Lee Grant as Felicia and Jack Warden as Felicia's adulterous husband, Lester. The story revolves around several days in the life of George Roundy, centred on 4 November 1968, election day, as Richard Nixon storms home to victory over Hubert Humphrey, with the television coverage providing background chatter.

George styles Jackie's hair for the banquet, which turns out to be a fiasco as his infidelity is revealed. Indeed, the hairstyles of the time were one of the film's points of interest on its release more than half a decade later. Christie goes from streaked hair falling in curls below the shoulder, part of a sexy but rather flashy and superficial look, to blonde, shoulder-length bob, giving her a more classic style hinting at maturity and sophistication. However, at the banquet, Jackie, Jill and Felicia discover they all have the same basic hairstyle. Although George is later seen pounding away on top of Jackie, she then dumps him, as does his wife. He loses all of his women and realizes that he is the one who has been used.

'I felt Julie, and Goldie also, made the picture work for me,' Beatty told Norman Mailer years later, 'and particularly the ending of *Shampoo* with Julie—that was after our relationship. The integrity on that face. That person. It's never faltered.'

Respected American critic Pauline Kael, writing in the *New Yorker*, contended that Christie was as charismatic as ever. 'In *Shampoo* she's not only an actress,' wrote Kael, 'she is—in the high-class-hooker terms of her role—the sexiest woman in movies right now. She has the knack of turning off her spirituality totally; in this role she's a gorgeous, whory-tipped little beast, a dirty sprite.' The trade paper *Variety* noted, 'Christie handles her role with ease and flair, and her final dismissal of Beatty is, by itself as well as in tandem with Hawn's, a dramatic highlight.'

Although some reviewers believed that *Shampoo* was hampered by its basic story, it proved to be another box-office success for Beatty as a producer and earned Columbia Pictures more money than any other film to that date. After Christie, Beatty, Hawn and Grant had all been nominated for Golden Globe awards, there was some consternation in Hollywood when, in January 1976, none of them turned up at the ceremony. Columbia subsequently issued a statement explaining

181

that Beatty had 'flu, Hawn was nursing her sick boyfriend, Grant didn't like awards and Christie had dashed off to London.

Very different from her previous pictures, *Shampoo* was certainly a satisfactory addition to Christie's list of film credits. She was happy to extend that further by agreeing to make a guest appearance as herself in Robert Altman's celebrated epic *Nashville*, set in the capital of Tennessee, having previously worked with the director on *McCabe & Mrs Miller*.

The film, written by Altman and Joan Tewkesbury and set in the American bicentennial year of 1976, provides a kaleidoscopic view of the country music capital of the world and the dreamers trying to make it there, including many eccentrics. The 1970 Oscar-winning documentary *Woodstock* had given a revealing insight into a rock festival, but *Nashville* captured the nature of a special type of music and those who were drawn to it. The drama was also intended to be a small picture of what was happening in American society as a whole, with the apparent death of the American Dream. 'What I found there was a place coming of age and losing its innocence,' said Tewkesbury. 'There were new drugs and one of the stars of the Grand Ole Opry had just been murdered. The music was changing, the culture was changing. It was a perfect place to capture the change that was going on in America.'

The story featured twenty-four main characters, played by stars such as Lily Tomlin, Ned Beatty, Keith Carradine, Karen Black and Jeff Goldblum, acting out half-a-dozen stories over 157 minutes, with many original songs performed. Geraldine Chaplin acted an emaciated groupie who claims to be a BBC television reporter and Christie's friend Shelley Duvall played another groupie. Like Christie, actor Elliott Gould appeared as himself, after previously starring in Altman films such as *M*A*S*H* and *The Long Goodbye.*

In the story, Christie is introduced to some of the characters at a darkened venue, including 'the grand old man of country music' Haven Hamilton (played by another Altman veteran, Henry Gibson), who has recorded his salute to the bicentennial, 'We Must Be Doing Something Right to Last 200 Years'. Hamilton says, rather banally, 'I was talking about The Christy Minstrels, and now we have Julie Christie.' After failing to recognize Christie and being told who she is, Karen Black's character, Connie White, exclaims, 'You mean she's a star, with *that* hairdo?' Both lines are almost lost in the din of conversation.

The onstage and backstage stories are acted out against the backdrop of a fictitious political campaign, with a Replacement Party candidate—never seen—aiming to become president. His team persuades some of the country music stars to take part in a political rally, which ends with the assassination of Nashville's most popular female singer.

After Christie's experience on the real-life political campaign trail and acting in *Shampoo*, the theme seemed familiar. The film came at an important time in American political history, following Watergate and the final withdrawal of troops from Vietnam. Although set in 1976, *Nashville* was released in the United States in the summer of the previous year and received rave reviews and recognition of its relevance to society.

Just as Americans were asking themselves about their country, Christie appeared to be jaded with life there and returned to Britain shortly before *Nashville*'s release. She was reported to have turned down a starring role alongside Dustin Hoffman and Laurence Olivier in *Marathon Man*, directed by John Schlesinger, one of her early mentors.

Entering another period of being choosy about which films she would act in, Christie— by now the owner of an American house on Dog Beach, between the Pacific and Malibu Canyon—re-established her British roots by buying a smallholding in a village near the Mid Wales town of Montgomery as a retreat from her London home and closer to her mother in Llanafan. Christie also moved her London base from a house in South Kensington to a one-bedroom flat in Notting Hill Gate. In August 1975, she was spotted having dinner with Warren Beatty in Leith's, a nearby west London restaurant, but all this seemed to prove only that they had remained friends long after their relationship had broken down.

Shortly afterwards, Christie was lined up to star with Donald Sutherland again in *The Petersburgh-Cannes Express*, scripted by Allan Scott and Chris Bryant, who were responsible for the screenplay of *'Don't Look Now'*. French director Claude Chabrol was due to make the film, planned as another Anglo-Italian co-production, but finance was not forthcoming and the idea was abandoned.

By the spring of 1976, Christie was back in the United States to film the futuristic thriller *Demon Seed*, which earned her a reported $250,000. Producer Herb Jaffe, offering her a car to drive during filming at MGM Studios in Culver City, California, and several Los Angeles locations, was surprised that she asked for only a Volkswagen with a stick shift, although this fitted in with Christie's remote existence in Wales, minimalistic way of life and gypsy-style clothes. Sticking to her principles, she did not make a show of having money and showed concern for those in need, although it was not until the 1980s that this would come to the fore more publicly.

In *Demon Seed*, though, Christie consciously decided no longer to put herself completely in the hands of 'paternalistic' directors. 'I'm no longer the little girl letting Daddy do all the work,' she explained later. 'With *Demon Seed*, I had to take a lot of responsibility, otherwise it would have turned into something I would not have cared to be in.'

Christie acted scientist's wife Susan Harris, who is raped by a computer that is intent on reproducing itself in human form. It had echoes of *A for Andromeda*, the television series that launched Christie on her screen career. Based on horror writer Dean R. Koontz's novel of the same name, *Demon Seed* also featured Robert Vaughn—Napoleon Solo in the popular 1960s television series *The Man from U.N.C.L.E.*—as the voice of the computer, Proteus IV, which was designed by Alex Harris (Fritz Weaver).

The critical scene in which the machine impregnates psychologist Susan with its artificially constructed sperm, after making her a hostage in her own home, is depicted by swirling abstract images. This 'cosmic voyage', believed to be the first visual representation of a computer's consciousness, transports Christie's character through landscapes of time and space.

However, on the film's release in 1977, the special effects, Donald Cammell's direction and the screenplay by Robert Jaffe and Roger O. Hirson—seen by some as literate, others as laughable—failed to win over audiences, who were keener to be taken into the world inhabited by *Star Wars*, which was also released that year. Film critic Alexander Walker described *Demon Seed* as '*Rosemary's Baby* mated with *2001: A Space Odyssey*', alluding to the implanting of an inhuman infant in a mother's womb in the first and the emergence of a flawed super-computer in the second.

Despite the lukewarm public response, Christie again graced a film with its most accomplished performance, giving integrity to the story without resorting to 'starry' acting. 'Miss Christie is too sensible an actress to be able to look frightened under the circumstances of her imprisonment,' wrote Vincent Canby in the *New York Times*. 'Most of the time she just looks bloody impatient, as the computer, with the help of an automated wheelchair and electric eyes that open and close doors, keeps her prisoner, makes medical tests on her and busies himself with creating his own—are you ready?—demon seed.' Joseph Gelmis, reviewing the film for the American publication *Newsday*, contended, 'The sight of Julie Christie trussed spreadeagle on her bed while a mechanical arm clinically handles her body is pure exploitation, as perverse as something out of the prurient feelies of *Brave New World*. It is a mistake, in an otherwise above average sci-fi film.'

The cinema trailer for the film was a collector's piece in itself, with a booming voice repeatedly intoning, 'Julie Christie carries the demon seed. Fear for her!' This was included when the picture was released on video in 1996, the year in which Donald Cammell—who had previously co-directed *Performance* with Nicolas Roeg—committed suicide.

Cinemagoers were more interested in Christie's screen performance when she was reunited with Warren Beatty in the romantic fantasy *Heaven Can Wait*, a remake of the 1941 picture *Here Comes Mr Jordan*. She played Betty Logan, who falls for Beatty's character, ageing American footballer Joe Pendleton. The sportsman is killed in a road accident before a big game, and on his way to Heaven his celestial messenger and the archangel Mr Jordan realize that he has been taken too soon. So, because his body has been cremated already, his spirit is transported back to Earth in the body of an eccentric millionaire industrialist recently murdered by his wife and secretary.

In the original picture, based on Harry Segall's play *Heaven Can Wait*, Robert Montgomery and Evelyn Keyes starred as the lovers, with Claude Rains taking the role of Mr Jordan, acted here by British star James Mason. Beatty, wearing his producer's hat, acquired the film rights for $25,000 from Jed Harris, a once successful New York stage director. He considered casting legendary world heavyweight champion Muhammad Ali to star as a boxer, as in the original play, but Ali was not available, so he resolved to take the lead role himself. As a result, he made the leading character a footballer and collaborated on the script with Elaine May. After talks with director Peter Bogdanovich broke down, Beatty decided to direct the film himself for the first time but, aware that he was also starring in it, brought in Buck Henry as co-director.

Christie joined Beatty, Mason and the other leading players, Jack Warden (who played Christie's married lover in *Shampoo*), Charles Grodin and Dyan Cannon, for filming around Los Angeles and at the Filoli Estate near San Jose, California, which had been handed over to the National Trust for Historic Preservation in 1975. The 35-acre estate, half of which was taken up with spectacular gardens, was home to a 45-room mansion typifying modified Georgian revival architecture.

Before shooting started on the film in the second half of 1977, Beatty had split up with Michelle Phillips and there was inevitable speculation that he and Christie might reunite. However, there were reports from the set that she refused to kiss him in a particular scene because it was not in her contract, as well as rumours that he argued with Cannon and she refused to take his direction. These were neither confirmed nor denied, but *Time* magazine critic Frank Rich commented on the 'touching romance between the hero and co-star Julie Christie, who communicate largely through passionate eye contact, the heat of which has not been felt since Clark Gable and Vivien Leigh met in *Gone with the Wind*'.

Outside the studio, the liveliest action came at the Los Angeles Coliseum in front of 60,000 American football fans, who had turned up to watch an exhibition game between the Los Angeles Rams and the Oakland Raiders. They were treated to the half-time spectacle of a Super Bowl sequence shot for the film, featuring Beatty as a quarterback alongside a team that also boasted half-a-dozen former Rams players.

Christie herself held up filming after breaking a wrist, while rollerskating off set. However, *Heaven Can Wait* was completed, and on its release in 1978 the picture proved to be Beatty's greatest success to date, eventually taking more than $120 million at box offices worldwide, although as an actor he appeared more lightweight. The film never won any Oscars, but it received ten nominations.

The broken wrist meant that Christie had to pull out of a role in *Agatha*, director Michael Apted's intriguing and speculative account of what might have happened to mystery writer Agatha Christie during her famous eleven-day disappearance in 1926. With time for reflection, Christie returned to Britain and left Hollywood behind. Her years with Beatty were over, the films she made there were a mixed bunch and her own political awareness and concerns for social issues were maturing. She said:

I never *chose* to work in America. It has never been my ambition to work in America. I was doing *Uncle Vanya* in the theatre in America and a film offer turned up and there was some sort of obligation and I had to do it. Then, with *Demon Seed*, I thought the idea was interesting and the film could be interesting, too . . . but it didn't turn out in a way I'd wanted it to. I still think it is an interesting idea. So I never really chose to do American films—they just came about—and I decided I had better take a hold of myself or I would be doing more American films. I didn't want to, I never have been interested in them.

Men seemed a bigger factor in Christie's decision to spend so much time in the United States, and she admitted that there were other lovers apart from Beatty. 'I simply went where my heart was and my work,' she explained. 'And Warren was just one of the "hearts". There was quite a lot of heart business in America besides Warren. America is a big country . . .'
She confessed that her return to Britain coincided with a time when there were no

191

lovers in her life. 'When one relationship was breaking up very unhappily and there didn't seem to be another one around the corner, I went back to England,' Christie explained. 'I'd never been content in America.'

One lasting friendship she made during her time there was with Shelley Duvall, who played one of Christie's 'girls' in *McCabe & Mrs Miller*. 'Julie was my first true friend in Hollywood,' said Duvall later. 'She was wonderful. You could trust her completely. I met her on *McCabe & Mrs Miller*, when we were filming in Canada, and then later knew her when she lived in a tiny beach house in Los Angeles. That was after her Warren period. She was always a lot of fun. We could talk for hours, be real serious, then laugh ourselves silly. She is smart and honest and very strong for what she believes in.'

Back home, Christie admitted to feeling a culture shock after so long away, in a different society. 'Having lived in Beverly Hills, I was very grateful to come home and see old women looking like old women, with little coats on and shopping bags, instead of being made-up, jewelled and label-dressed.'

From 1978, Christie's Welsh cottage became a more permanent base, away from the glitz and glamour of the film world. Although on the surface becoming a recluse, she could map out her life from that small haven of peace. She could choose when to cast herself in front of the public on screen or as a campaigner for social justice, before returning to shut herself away in her idyllic home.

CHAPTER FOURTEEN

PEOPLE, POLITICS AND PICTURES

Back on her own side of the Atlantic, Christie signalled a move away from the mainstream by accepting a starring role with Jacques Perrin in the French film *Sophie et le Capitaine*, and turning down the lead role, opposite John Travolta, in *American Gigolo*. Lauren Hutton stepped in to keep the Hollywood producers happy, but Travolta himself eventually pulled out and was replaced by Richard Gere before filming began. Hollywood no longer appeared to hold any fascination for Christie.

Instead, for the first time since acting in *Fahrenheit 451* for François Truffaut, she was able to work with a French director, this time in a French-backed production made in that country. But, after two weeks' shooting in June 1978, executive producer Irene Silberman cancelled *Sophie et le Capitaine*, accusing director Liliane de Kermadec of making the picture differently from the way it was planned.

Four months later, Christie, who was paid

her fee for the film, made a special visit to Paris for a press conference called by the French Film Directors' Association. Sitting next to de Kermadec, she voiced her support for the director. 'As far as I was concerned,' Christie told journalists, 'Liliane was filming exactly the picture in which I had agreed to act. It was a formidable experience for me to find such a talent as hers. It is important that the cinema should not lose talents like that.' Christie also attacked the way in which the film had been axed. 'I consider that I have been badly treated,' she said. 'I have never before heard of such conditions being imposed on an actor. As with every actor, I work with the director of the film and, if there is any problem, it is with the director that I discuss and solve it. It is scandalous that an actor, engaged by both a producer and a director, should be dismissed by the producer without consultation with the director.'

Christie returned from Paris to join the new man in her life, investigative journalist Duncan Campbell, at a tenth-anniversary party for his magazine, *Time Out*, at the Lyceum, in London. Although she had been seen on the arm of former Roxy Music keyboards player Brian Eno for a short time, romance had blossomed with Scotsman Campbell over the preceding months and the London-magazine journalist was to become a permanent fixture in her life. They had holidayed in Peru during the summer of 1978 and continued to share time together at her cottage in Wales or either of their homes in London, but partnership clearly suited them more than marriage. This was in line with Christie's previous relationships, with Don Bessant and Warren Beatty; she had always questioned the need for couples to go through a ceremony confirming their love for one another.

The actress also enjoyed being surrounded by friends, especially creative ones, and in San Francisco had met a couple with whom she became very close. Artist Lesley Heale and her husband, Jonathan, himself an artist who had exhibited at several London galleries, agreed to move into Christie's Welsh farmhouse and look after it in her absence. The actress had sold off some of the acres around it but still had a pond in the front garden and bred rare geese.

It was here that her life was touched by tragedy, when, in March 1979, in an event chillingly reminiscent of the opening scene in 'Don't Look Now', the Heales' 22-month-old son, Harry, drowned in the two-foot-deep pond. He had been playing near his mother as she dug in the vegetable garden outside the house, and when he wandered off she presumed he had gone into a barn. However, by the time Christie and Campbell drove into the grounds, she realized that he was missing and they all launched a search for the toddler.

Eventually, his mother saw what looked like a grey rug floating towards the middle of the pond. Realizing that this was her son, Heale waded into the water, pulled Harry out and carried him into the house, where she and Christie tried to revive him as he lay motionless on the living-room settee. Two doctors and an ambulance crew arrived on the scene, but all attempts to save the toddler failed. Three days later, a coroner recorded a verdict of accidental death.

The apparent glitz and glamour of acting in front of a camera must have seemed a million miles away at this time. It was more than a year since Christie had completed her last film, *Heaven Can Wait*, and it would be another eighteen months before she started work on her next one. Whether in Wales or London, Christie took the opportunity to spend more time with friends. Journalist Michele Roberts, who worked alongside Duncan Campbell on *Time Out* and, later, *City Limits*, saw the actress at parties. 'On Christmas night, she and Duncan threw a party at his North London flat,' she recalled of one such occasion. 'Julie and Duncan had us all playing games, laughing, egging each other on to fresh absurdities. Julie raced about in a black minidress and black stockings, pressing wine and food on us. She dished out presents. She gossiped and joked. She made everybody feel welcome and special. She's got that kind of charm. She didn't care when her stockings laddered. She carried on weaving the party together and enabling everybody to enjoy themselves.'

But more sadness came into Christie's life in March 1982 with the sudden death of her mother, from a heart attack, at the age of sixty-nine. Rosemary Christie had enjoyed her years in Wales, with son Clive living in a nearby village and daughter Julie further across, towards the English border. She and her partner, Douglas Hague, were noted for their archaeological and conservation work, particularly in recording the lights and watch towers of British and other European coasts on sometimes perilous sea or air journeys.

Rosemary and Hague, a divorcé, had never seen the need to exchange vows, but he did later marry a second time. On his death from cancer in 1990, Hague left to the National Library of Wales an archive of material that he had collected with Rosemary Christie for a planned book on lighthouses. He also bequeathed to Julie Christie four of his large sketchbooks and a Calais lighthouse painting, and to Clive 'my Russian Triptych, my black Shellelagh and my laboratory balance'. Hague was buried in the same grave as Rosemary Christie, in the churchyard at Llanafan, along with her favourite handbag.

*   *   *

The 1980s was a decade when Christie gave her public support to social and political causes, and became even more discerning in her choice of films, most of them thought-provoking and low-budget, but often too downbeat to appeal to wide audiences.

She had already helped a campaign to protest about nuclear power, back in 1977, before making *Heaven Can Wait*, although the title of that film seemed as far away from the truth as possible in view of the dangers she vocalized. 'I have a retiring nature and I never usually give interviews,' she said at the time. 'But this subject is so vital for everybody that I feel I must take a stand.' The issue was the decision about to be made by the British government on whether to turn the world's nuclear waste into plutonium, the raw material of the nuclear bomb, using the new reactor at Windscale, Cumbria (later renamed Sellafield).

Christie spent much time briefing herself on the issue, going through books, newspaper cuttings and scientific magazines, saying she was concerned to warn of the dangers of this deadly material. She pointed out that the government's case for going ahead with nuclear power was backed by lawyers and experts who were paid with taxpayers' money, whereas those who exercised their democratic right and questioned the move had no public funds to draw on. Over the next few years, she lent her support to a new group called Pandora (People Against Nuclear Dumping On Rural Areas), and put her energies into helping the movement by taking part in basic chores such as collecting signatures from those opposed to the government's plans.

Apart from going on the American presidential campaign trail with Warren Beatty, this was Christie's first experience of using her fame to publicize social issues about which she was concerned. However, she was in no way the typical star attaching her name to the latest cause and doing little else. Throughout the 1980s, she did not tire of campaigning on various issues, including opposition to nuclear weapons, American interference in Nicaragua and the denial of aid to Cambodia after Pol Pot's genocide.

Those who simply regarded her as left-wing had to contend with the fact that when she joined the campaign against nuclear power, for example, she lined up against a British Labour government. Wherever her personal vote went, her campaigns were socially, not politically, motivated. In the 1960s, she had declared herself a socialist. Now she simply described her politics as liberal.

Christie credited her years with Warren Beatty for helping to open her eyes to political issues. 'It was a wonderful learning period,' she recalled. 'I had access to politics through

Warren—and power. He opened a door which has never shut and understanding power is something I am very grateful to him for. I wouldn't have searched it out for myself, but it is very useful to know and to see how people you might loathe and despise and hate operate as human beings. That is very interesting, especially for an actor.'

She became vocal in her support for CND at a time when it was enjoying a revival because of concern over the build-up of nuclear weapons. In April 1981 Christie was one of the speakers at a Ban the Bomb rally at Newbury, in Berkshire, just two miles from Greenham Common, where American Cruise missiles were due to be sited and women set up a peace camp. Four months later, she told 4,000 peace marchers in Paris, 'We must fight against both Russian and American nuclear bombs and support an independent denuclearized Europe.'

In 1984 Christie travelled to Washington and New York with members of the Women's Peace Alliance from five European countries to demand that America cease deploying nuclear missiles in their countries. They met Richard H. Burt, the assistant secretary of state for European affairs, members of Congress and Paul Nitze, America's chief negotiator in the stalled intermediate-range nuclear arms talks. 'I have never wanted to be involved in politics at all, but I couldn't resist the ecological issues,' Christie said at a press conference. 'Then, I came to realize that politics is inextricably linked to everything I feel strongly about.'

Christie followed through her principles by starring in the film *Memoirs of a Survivor*, based on Doris Lessing's novel about the disintegration of society in urban Britain, complete with food shortages and marauding gangs. The action takes place possibly in the aftermath of a nuclear holocaust, although this is not explained. Christie accepted a small fee for her role, with a percentage of profits to come if the picture proved a success. She also narrated a 1983 television documentary, *Taking on the Bomb*, in Channel Four's *Broadside* series, about the peace movement in Europe and the mobilization of opinion among women. During the British general election four years later, Christie joined other campaigners on the CND Express, a double-decker bus setting off from London to spread the nuclear disarmament message around forty-four marginal constituencies.

Memoirs of a Survivor, Christie's first film in three years, was directed by David Gladwell, who wrote the screenplay with Kerry Crabbe, and it was considered that she would give the picture a good chance at the box office. Gladwell had initially approached French actress Jeanne Moreau, then in her early fifties, to play the role. 'I went to see her because she was nearer the age of the character,' he recalled, 'but Mamoun Hassan from British Screen, which put money into the production, was very keen on Julie and it was considered that she would probably be best for the project.'

Christie's agent was sent the script, but before reading it Christie viewed Gladwell's debut feature, *Requiem for a Village*. Produced by the British Film Institute in 1975, the picture was about the changing way of rural life; she was impressed by the director's individual style. 'So I read the script, couldn't really understand it, but thought it was an intelligent script anyway,' explained Christie. 'It wasn't being stupid or any of the other things that they often are.' She insisted that *Memoirs of a Survivor* was a fairy story, not a political film, but the issue of nuclear weapons and the potentially disastrous results of them were clearly close to her heart.

In the picture, set in the near-future, Christie starred as a middle-aged woman known only as D, who passes through the wall of her flat into Victorian times to escape the destruction and anarchy all around her. There she finds a middle-class family whose affluence hides their own desolation of spirit. The girl of the family, Emily, is mirrored in another Emily billeted on D, both of them resisting the 'old' and 'new' societies in this allegory.

Wearing grubby, ill-fitting clothes and a wig,

Christie threw herself into the character of this dowdy woman, surveying the devastation as she pushes a pram filled with tins of food that she has scavenged. Anarchy rules as survivors of the disaster head north to 'safe' areas, with debris and uncollected rubbish bags littering the streets. David Gladwell said:

Julie needed to be very involved. She wouldn't just be a jobbing actress and do as she was told. She wanted to have some say in the development of the character. The role was passive and Julie wasn't called on to do much apart from being there, witnessing everything going on round about her, rather like Malcolm McDowell in *O Lucky Man!* So she decided what activities she should be doing while all this was happening, such as upholstering a chair. She always felt it absolutely necessary to be doing something active and useful, which at the beginning I didn't feel would be necessary. Probably wrongly, I would have been quite happy with her just observing. She was least happy in the scenes in which she goes through the wall, where she simply had to be an observer and couldn't do things.

During filming in Norwich, an extra who appeared as one of the refugees noticed how Christie nevertheless maintained a low-key presence. 'The scene is Julie Christie seeing the "fugitives" pack up and move on past her tower block home,' recorded Kingsley Canham in his diary. 'Julie Christie does an almost unnoticed rehearsal of her walk past us, then we shoot it in another four takes . . . She moves back quickly between the first and second takes, then more slowly in the latter takes, seemingly absorbed totally in the action, presenting a lonely figure.' Canham also noted that Christie was, amusingly, accosted by a local. 'An elderly Norwich citizen who has been observing the proceedings with disgust approaches her, apparently abusing her for being personally responsible for the litter strewn around the set,' he wrote. 'Her response goes unrecorded.'

In between filming scenes, Christie made an impression on Leonie Mellinger, who acted Emily, as someone who cared deeply about humanitarian issues. 'One could sense that Julie was extremely aware of things that were going on at the time and she would scour the newspapers daily, circling certain things that were of interest,' recalled Mellinger. 'She would discuss issues, but it wasn't like she was sitting there holding forth about her views. She wasn't trying to press anybody over anything. I remember we went on a march during the time that the film was being made.'

However, those who did not share Christie's views found her politics slightly hard to take.

'She had a bee in her bonnet about lots of ecological issues,' recalled director of photography Walter Lassally's agent, Kate Campbell, who was on the set throughout filming. 'She preached her views rather more than some people who worked with her thought to be acceptable. At every available moment, she could turn the tide of a conversation to whatever issue she was into. She's always carrying a cross for something, but it's boring.'

John Altman, who played a revolutionary in the film before finding television fame as villainous Nick Cotton in *EastEnders*, found Christie and her concerns far from boring. 'As a kid, I had seen her in *Darling*, *Doctor Zhivago*, *'Don't Look Now'* and other films,' Altman recalled. 'I always thought she was one of the greatest English screen stars and I always liked the mystery that surrounded her. She was beautiful but also had a great naturalism about her and what struck me when I walked on the set and met her was that she still had that. It was an absolute treat to have dinner in a hotel with her and some of the cast after filming. She was very relaxed and laid back, and clearly had a caring soul. I was totally charmed by her, really.'

In some ways, *Memoirs of a Survivor*—which received its world premiere at the Cannes Film Festival in May 1981—was in the socio-realistic tradition of 1960s British cinema, but the X-certificate film received mixed reviews on its release in Britain four months later. Actress Maria Aitken, acting as guest film critic in the *Daily Mail*, regarded it as 'evidence of the blossoming of the British film industry' and added, 'Julie Christie, shining with serenity and more beautiful than ever after four years' [sic] absence from the screen, is at her best.' Others remarked on the lack of complete devastation—'shortages but not starvation, distant disturbances but not complete breakdown' and D 'living fairly elegantly in a flat'.

Shortly after the film's release, Christie was also heard narrating—for free—another picture, a harrowing documentary entitled *The Animals Film*, showing the horrors perpetrated in the name of science and maximum productivity. It received its premiere at the National Film Theatre during the 1981 London Film Festival, where it received a standing ovation. The actress explained to journalists there that she had been a vegetarian for eleven years, since filming part of *The Go-Between* at a pig farm, and added that her concern for animals dated back to childhood. 'Unlike most children,' she said, 'I couldn't stand zoos. I could see they were like prison cells, with the animals pacing backwards and forwards looking bored or agitated. I hated circuses. It seemed so sad to see animals forced to respond in unnatural ways.'

Victor Schonfeld, the American producer, director and writer of *The Animals Film*, approached Christie to narrate it after spending two years gathering enough film material to put the documentary together. Initially she had her doubts. She said:

I suspected it would be a kind of Disney 'Let's be kind to the fluffy bunnies' type of thing. However, I went and saw and, gruelling experience though it was, I saw a film that reached to the roots of all our confusions about our treatment of animals. Because it's not about animals—it's about us. It's about human nature and the atrocities some factions of it can quite blandly commit. It's about the deadness of the mind that can commit these atrocities without blinking, every day, exactly in the same way they're being committed, for example, in El Salvador today. And it's about our participation in these atrocities even when we're not the perpetrators.

Christie pointed out that people who professed to love animals wore furs and make-up and ate food that was the direct result of cruelty to animals. 'I am very careful with make-up, cosmetics, soap and so on,' she explained, 'and always check whether animals are used in their production. But I can't avoid household products, like cleaning materials, that have caused hundreds of animals excruciating agony.'

Director Schonfeld, in his search for a celebrity narrator, had been persistent in his attempts to persuade Christie. 'I wrote to Julie in London, although I'd never met her, and basically just kept pursuing her,' he said. 'When she agreed, it was a fantastic breakthrough, and there couldn't have been a better choice.' In fact, she was also instrumental in persuading rock star Robert Wyatt to write the original score for the film.

In April 1982 Christie, wearing a black beret and brown battledress trousers, sat alongside two hooded animal-rights activists to promote the film when it went on general release in Britain. She spoke of the 'enormous sacrifice being made by the animals, which is the infliction of absolutely appalling pain on them, in order that we should have certain comforts or luxuries', adding that 'capitalism invents things that have to be made'.

Christie was prepared to court controversy by aligning herself with members of the Northern Animal Liberation League. Its members refused to be identified for fear of being prosecuted over the organization's break-ins at factory farms and research establishments. 'Maybe these tactics are the only way to make a dent in people's consciences,' she said. 'I'm not a very courageous person myself, so I don't know whether I would ever go on a raid. But I might be driven to it.'

The 136-minute documentary, which was made for £150,000, included a mixture of colour and black-and-white film from the United States and Britain of soldiers exposing animals to a nuclear blast, farmers de-beaking hens, hunters killing a deer and sharing out the heart and hooves as trophies, and surgeons using a grafting technique to create a two-headed dog. The film was at the centre of controversy itself when scheduled by Channel Four during the new station's first week on the air, in November 1982. The Independent Broadcasting Authority (IBA), which then regulated commercial television in Britain, objected to film of Northern Animal Liberation League members in training and breaking into a research laboratory. The IBA claimed that this material, as well as interviews with them and Animal Liberation Front activists, contravened the 1981 Broadcasting Act by inciting violence.

Schonfeld eventually agreed to cut five minutes from the final, twelve-minute sequence, which the IBA had originally wanted to be completely removed from the film. This compromise came after the director pointed out that the documentary had already been shown in cinemas with an AA certificate and Scotland Yard had viewed it without taking action. Furthermore, Schonfeld's sale to

Channel Four included a clause in the contract that no cuts would be made except in the case of any IBA objections, where he would have 'to discuss and implement cuts of a reasonable nature'. As a result, the film was broadcast with captions at the beginning explaining the IBA's action in ordering the deletion of 'sequences concerned with the ideas and activities of Militant Liberation Activists', as well as Schonfeld's reply: 'The film-makers have acceded, under protest, to the cuts. However, they maintain their belief that an honest portrayal of a political reality ought not to be prohibited under the law.'

The Animals Film made waves in other countries, too. In Australia, for instance, the New South Wales Department of Education sent members of its Film Exhibition Review Committee to see special screenings of the documentary in Sydney before its commercial release in that country. Instead of recommending that the film should be shown to schoolchildren of a certain age, or at least recommended to them, the department's director-general of education wrote to the cinema manager, 'I regret to advise that the film does not merit variation of the normal school routine for screening at matinée sessions during school hours. Schools will be advised of this recommendation.'

Nine years later, *The Animals Film* was screened again on British television, in

Channel Four's 'Banned' season, featuring films and television programmes that had experienced censorship. The Independent Television Commission, which had by then taken over the regulation of British commercial television, demanded that two interviews be cut from the concluding sequence of the original cinema version. In the end the documentary was broadcast without any commercial breaks because, explained Channel Four, of 'the powerful nature of many of the images in this film, depicting man's inhumanity towards animals'.

*   *   *

Christie's feminist views were to the fore when she accepted a role in *The Gold Diggers*. She had not aired these views publicly before, but they were the reason for her rejection of certain film roles in which the woman was simply an appendage to the male lead, or her story was acted out through him. 'That's what I object to, parts in which women do things through the male protagonists,' she said. 'Playing those sorts of roles can't change anything.'

Christie had read Germaine Greer's homage to feminism and female liberation, *The Female Eunuch*, in the United States in the early 1970s. A decade later she admitted that it had made her realize how women had been discriminated against. 'I'd taken it on faith that men were more intelligent than women,' she said. 'I now have very few men friends, it's nearly all women—because I find that it's the women who are developed and the men who aren't.'

So it was a coup for first-time feature-film director Sally Potter when Christie accepted the starring role in *The Gold Diggers*, which was made on location in Iceland by an all-woman cast and crew. Initially titled *Gold* and financed by the British Film Institute Production Board in association with Channel Four, the £250,000 picture was intended to show that women are not simply to be worshipped as a commodity. In the process, it aimed to rewrite cinema history from a feminist perspective.

Christie played Ruby, a white woman reliving her childhood in spartan conditions in icy Yukon country, where her entertainer father was a gold prospector. Unknown actress Colette Laffont took the role of Celeste, a black French bank employee in London trying to get information out of her patronizing bosses about the meaning of money and how it is controlled. The 'gold' found by both is the means to personal and political transformation, and provides a blueprint for social change.

Gold was firmly rooted in the tradition of British independent cinema, which had resulted in pictures that were rarely seen outside arthouse cinemas and film societies. However, recent changes to the financing of such productions meant that they could get bigger budgets and be screened more widely. That was certainly Potter's hope.

'Julie Christie was not vital to getting it into production,' she said before the film's release, 'but obviously her presence will help it get shown to a wider audience than might otherwise have been the case. But the main thing that makes her so interesting is that she is the perfect vehicle for the point of the script. Her presence makes the connection between the glamour of the mainstream film world and the criticism of it we are trying to put across.'

Using only female technicians proved a difficult ambition to fulfil because of the small number of experienced women in some fields, caused by the lack of opportunities that the male-dominated film industry had created—one point that Potter wanted the picture to make. However, the presence of New York-based French director of photography Babette Mangolte was a great boon because of her talent for filming landscapes. The use of black-and-white photography throughout gave the picture a particularly dramatic look and gelled well with its depiction of early cinema films.

Recruiting female costume-makers and designers was easy and there were enough women sound technicians to choose from, but lighting technicians who worked on the film came from the theatre, with special dispensation from the union ACTT. Similarly, the set builders had either trained as carpenters on government-funded TOPS courses or came from fringe theatre or the performance arts.

All the cast and crew accepted a wage of just £30 a day, and that included Christie, who described it as 'the most satisfying film I've ever worked on'. She added:

> It makes an amazing difference being just with women. In all my other films, almost everyone around me was male. It's a slightly lonely position, which you tackle by bantering and creating a sort of bonhomie. It's a very flirtatious situation . . . There are all sorts of odd things you can do with your own sex which you don't do when there's a man around, even something as trivial as lifting up your skirt and scratching your behind when you feel like it. All the censoring you did when you were with men was unnecessary. Language, behaviour, everything was uncensored.

During filming in Iceland, the cast and crew endured extremely tough conditions. They began by trekking into the mountains, erecting a small but heavy portable hut there and waiting for moments of sun to film in. A simple panning shot round a frozen landscape involved driving in a convoy through turbulent rivers, battling through blizzards and holding down a tripod in gale-force winds. But the feeling that they were doing something to further the feminist cause, and perhaps change attitudes, generated a bonhomie and sense of adventure in all those making the film.

Tracey Eddon, Christie's stunt double for two scenes of Ruby on horseback shot in Britain, recalled the atmosphere of the production as different from anything else she had worked on. 'It was very quiet—there was no screaming and shouting,' she said. 'The only men were the caterers and a few extras. Apart from that it was all women, and it was lovely. Everything got done just the same as in other films but without any dramas.'

By the time the picture received its world premiere at the National Film Theatre, London, in May 1984, three years after work had begun on it, the title had changed to *The Gold Diggers*. Reaction to the film from the mainstream press was predictable, particularly criticisms that it caricatured men, but director Potter—who went on to make *Orlando* and *The Man Who Cried*—considered that this only balanced 'the mockery of women in so many commercial features'.

Christie continued to lend her support to the women's movement by travelling to Washington in 1985 for the annual festival

215

staged by the Women in Film and Video organization based there. Two years after its release in Britain, Christie's film *The Return of the Soldier* received its American premiere at the festival, so she was accompanied by co-star Ann-Margret, producer Ann Skinner and production designer Luciana Arrighi. 'I knew Ann when she was John Schlesinger's continuity girl, many years ago,' said Christie. 'She was always very impressive. But I certainly had no idea that inside her lay a driving producer—and driving is what you have to be. There are hardly any women producers in Britain.'

The portrayal of women on screen was also a factor in Christie's admiration of films made in mainland Europe and, in particular, actresses Delphine Seyrig, Nathalie Baye and Hanna Schygulla. 'It's not just that they take their craft seriously, but they seem to force us into thinking about definitions of women,' said Christie. 'They present more than images; they give us a psychology of a type of woman and continue to develop that throughout a career.'

The press and public were becoming used to hearing or reading of Christie's concerns. She was reported to have put money into *City Limits*, the London magazine set up by former *Time Out* journalists, including Duncan Campbell. It was no surprise, either, when, in February 1983, the actress presented *Why Their News Is Bad News*, an episode in BBC2's

216

public access 'Open Door' series, championing the cause of the Campaign for Press and Broadcasting Freedom. With actress Julie Walters, she presented examples of allegedly biased reporting by television news and questioned its claim to be impartial. For its part, the press portrayed Christie as a child of the 1960s who had settled down to a reclusive rural life—a woman concerned more with putting forward her political views than making films. Although she shied away from most of the media, the actress was happy to let the short-lived *News on Sunday*—conceived as a popular paper of the Left—photograph her in the living-room of her Welsh cottage, holding one of her two Indian Runner ducks, in 1987.

Christie's interests in seeing justice done led her to join the 'shadow board' of Barclays Bank, a group of anti-apartheid campaigners formed in the early 1980s to highlight the bank's activities in South Africa. Other 'board' members included former South African newspaper editor Donald Woods—whose friendship with black civil rights leader Steve Biko was immortalized in director Richard Attenborough's film *Cry Freedom*—two MPs and clergymen, including the Rt Rev Stanley Booth-Clibbon, Bishop of Manchester. Each year, this group published a 'balance sheet' detailing Barclays' increased support for the Pretoria regime.

CHAPTER FIFTEEN

WAR ZONES

—

One part of the world that received particular attention from Christie was Nicaragua, where the American-backed right-wing dictator Anastasio Somoza had been overthrown by the Sandinistas in 1979. The new regime put education and health at the top of its list of priorities for rejuvenating the small Central American country, where thousands had been killed by Somoza's death squads, and poverty, disease and illiteracy were rife. Meanwhile, President Reagan, after taking office in 1981, started financing the Contra rebels, who sought to bring the old order back to power, and supplied American 'advisers' to train them. Christie declared the revolution 'worthwhile, just for the people to become human beings', adding, 'I've got no words for what's happening in Nicaragua now. It's almost impossible to talk about the savagery of the richest, most powerful country in the world financing those national guardsmen in the Contras.'

Despite her commitment to justice in Nicaragua, Christie turned down an offer to star as a radio reporter in the 1983 American film *Under Fire*. This also featured Nick Nolte as an American war photographer covering the cataclysmic events of 1979, who abandons any pretence of impartiality by putting his weight behind the Sandinistas as they are about to begin their last push on the capital, Managua. The actress felt that the female reporter's job was overshadowed by her relationship with the photographer. 'It seemed to me that her relationship was with her man, not her work,' said Christie.

It proved to be a bad decision because the film, the first to be made by British director Roger Spottiswoode, managed to combine an intelligent political thriller based on real-life events with a screen romance between Nolte and Joanna Cassidy, the American actress who eventually took the part turned down by Christie. On its completion, *Under Fire* was widely acclaimed at European film festivals, which in itself would have been been a recommendation to the actress. 'I think I made a mistake,' Christie conceded after the film's release. 'But maybe that's because Joanna Cassidy has brought something to the part that I couldn't see in the script.'

During 1983, Christie joined a star-studded cast that included comedians Ben Elton, Rik Mayall and French and Saunders, as well as actors and actresses Kenneth Cranham, Alfred Molina, Charlotte Cornwell and Emma Thompson, at the Shaftesbury Theatre, London, for *An Evening for Nicaragua*. The benefit concert, with the stars giving their services free, was in aid of the mass-literacy programme being carried out in the country. Highlights from the show were broadcast in Britain on Channel Four.

The next year, Christie visited Nicaragua twice, the first time with a British cultural delegation that also included playwright David Hare, poet Roger Woddis and actor Andy de la Tour. They were greeted by a welcoming concert in the shell of Managua's Grand Hotel, which had been devastated by an earthquake twelve years earlier, in the absence of any other suitable venues. Poetry and sculpture were among the arts booming in the years after Nicaragua's popular revolution, and Christie's meeting with the head of the Ministry of Culture, Father Ernesto Cardenal, a Nobel Prize-winning poet, left a marked impression on the actress. Remarking on one of his poems comparing Marilyn Monroe's body to a temple peopled by the merchants driven out by Jesus, she said, 'He understands so well the exploitation of the female image for profit.'

Christie expressed her admiration for poetry workshops, including some for the police and army, and the country's twenty-six Centres for Popular Culture, backed by the Ministry of Culture, which held workshops in painting, music and theatre. 'I think there's a terrific scorn of culture in Britain,' she said, 'a kind of philistinism that you don't get in France, for instance.' After her trips to Nicaragua, Christie declared that she had enjoyed visiting the country more than she had expected, having previously 'thought it was going to be too totalitarian for my liberal views'.

In an attempt to join direct action against President Reagan's policy towards Nicaragua, Christie took part in a demonstration outside the Guildhall, in London, during one of his visits, in 1988. Others taking part included British actor Jeremy Irons. However, police averted a confrontation by parking a van in front of the demonstrators.

By early 1985, after another break of more than two years from making films, Christie proclaimed that maybe she had been too choosy about her screen roles, having turned down three American productions during the first half of the decade. 'I think I've decided to stop being so fussy,' she said. 'There was always some reason or another. Either I thought the woman character was slightly insulting to women of her sort, or else the film was about something abroad and there'd be that awful thing by which a country and a race become background for the European white carrying-ons. Now I've decided, just screw it, and just be part of it all. If you want to be perfect—ideologically perfect, that is—you can just tie yourself up into a little knot.'

During 1985, Christie made the American film *Power*, although that and her subsequent features, *Miss Mary* and *La Mémoire Tatouée*—set in South America and North Africa respectively—still seemed to embrace the qualities that had previously made her so discerning in her choice of pictures. *Power*, also starring Richard Gere, was the only one of the three that could be described as mainstream and even that was about political manipulation of the media.

In January 1986 Christie arrived in Buenos Aires to play the title role of an 'English' governess of the late 1930 in *Miss Mary*. The Falklands War of four years earlier was still firmly rooted in the memories of the British, who ousted the Argentine junta's troops after they invaded the islands in pursuit of a historical claim to them. 'I want to show England's huge influence on Argentina's higher class, through the education that successive generations received from those inexorable British pedagogues,' announced Christie on her arrival at Buenos Aires airport, where she said it made no sense for Argentina and Britain to remain enemies.

Argentine feminist director María Luisa Bemberg's English-language film revolves around the authoritarianism of the upper classes in that country in the years leading to Juan Perón's popular success. As Mary Mulligan, the prim, sexually repressed heroine,

222

Christie portrayed an Irish Catholic desperately seeking the stability and security that is disappearing from her own world as the Empire crumbles and Britain heads towards war with Hitler.

What Miss Mary finds is a patriarchal man, Alfredo, who cheats on his subservient wife, Mecha, by seducing widow Perla and causing the disintegration of his family, as she (Mary) supervises the raising of his three children. However, the temptation to succumb to sex with the elder son, Johnny (played by Donald McIntire), as he grows older leads to Miss Mary's dismissal in 1945, the year in which Peron assumed power in Argentina and Britain emerged victorious from the Second World War.

The director drew on her own experience of governesses living far from home and captured the period feel by including the music of Duke Ellington, Benny Goodman and others on the soundtrack, while director of photography Miguel Rodriguez's images of the Argentine landscape gave Miss Mary an authentic look. 'I was going to call her Miss Maggie,' Bemberg said of the title character, 'but Julie Christie said no, you can't do that, it's going to be interpreted as Mrs Thatcher, who's much more vicious than dear old Miss Mary.'

Christie researched her role enthusiastically, reading books about the lives of governesses and nannies. She said:

There seem to have been roughly two kinds. There was the adventuress sort, who might not have been at all sexually repressed but would still have to pass on a dignified model to her charges. They were lively enough to enliven the places they entered. A lot of the other 'Miss Mary' sort had repressed their sexuality completely and saw it as their duty to pass on that repression as an aspect of the civilized education. There seems to have been an awful lot of women who clearly had no healthy relationship to men.

Portraying the governess as a dowdy, middle-aged woman caused no problems for Christie, as it might have done for other big-name actresses. 'I wanted her to look plain, lacking that light . . . that people have who are aware of their own sexuality,' she said. 'From that came all sorts of other things: her carriage, the way she wore her hair. It was difficult, though, to feel what it was like to have repressed all your possibilities.'

The actress acknowledged that the people's hero worship for Perón had to be tempered by the reality that in later years he was repressive. 'One of the most important lessons I learned there was to avoid being too quick to judge other nations' political predilections, even if they are utterly abhorrent to us,' said Christie. But she was concerned to hear of the continuing repression experienced by people in Argentina. 'A woman told me she'd been sent her daughter's hand in a jar,' said Christie. 'People have lived in terror for years and years—and they're experimenting with talking. A lot of the actors and actresses in the film have had very frightening experiences and had to go into exile. The military still has enormous power. It's a horrible situation with the debt on the one hand and the military on the other.'

Politics, and Christie's willingness to listen to the oppressed, was never far away from her work in the 1980s. After *Miss Mary*, which was premiered at the Venice Film Festival in September 1986 but did little business outside arthouse cinemas in Britain and other countries, her next port of call was Africa, to make the French-Tunisian production *La Mémoire Tatouée*.

Tunisian director Ridha Béhi had received the honour of having his film *Les Anges* included in the Directors Fortnight at the 1985 Cannes Film Festival. Now, in *La Mémoire Tatouée*, he cast Christie as Liverpudlian saloon-bar singer Betty. In 1955 she and husband Paul Rivière (played by American actor Ben Gazzara) both flee North Africa in a vintage Buick, on the eve of independence. Paul's illegitimate son, Wanis, has a crush on Betty, although it is not consummated, even when as an adult (a role taken by Algerian-born French actor Patrick Bruel) he later meets her again in a nightclub.

Once more, Christie was attracted to a film after enjoying one of the director's previous pictures. She explained:

I saw *Soleil de Hyènes* [*Sun of Hyenas*] some years ago. I adored that film. Therefore, when I learned that Rihda Béhi wanted to contact me, I said yes immediately without even looking at the script! This kind of cinema must not die. Countries like Tunisia have things to tell us. These are subjects the cinema never discusses. That interests me. You know, in my career, I have appeared in many big-budget productions, I've met great directors and enjoyed fame. Today, however, I'm trying to discover other attractions in the work.

She was also enthusiastic about travelling to Tunisia. 'About five years ago, I saw a good film about the effects of tourism on a Tunisian village,' Christie said shortly before making *La Mémoire Tatouée*. 'It was marvellous, since tourism is such a source of economic and social disruption in the world. Then, by a fluke, the director Ridha Béhi got hold of me to be in this film about colonialism. It's something to be excited about and I don't have to worry, as I would with a European director, about racism and balance and getting

Tunisians and the white colonialists right.'

Christie and Gazzara spoke in English, while the supporting cast was dubbed, as was Christie's singing voice, by jazz stars Chan Parker and Kim Parker. The script included metaphors such as Wanis's preoccupation with cars and, as a period drama, *La Mémoire Tatouée* held some interest. However, the film sank into oblivion and was not seen in cinemas at all in the United States, where it was released on video in 1989, under the title *Secret Obsession.*

Another forgotten production to which Christie gave her time, as narrator, was *Yilmaz Güney: His Life, His Films.* This British television documentary, commissioned by Channel Four, profiled the Turkish writer-director who, as an opponent of his country's repressive regime, used films as a political weapon. While they were being acclaimed abroad, at home he endured bans, censorship and imprisonment, often directing from jail by 'remote control'.

In 1984 producer-director Jane Cousins Mills had interviewed Güney only six weeks before his death and, with the help of film editor David Gladwell, who directed *Memoirs of a Survivor*, she mixed this with clips from his pictures. Güney, who grew up as a peasant in Turkish Kurdistan, had directed *Yol* from prison before escaping and fleeing to France, where the picture won the coveted Palme

227

D'Or at the Cannes Film Festival.

'Julie agreed to do the narration because of the political aspects,' said Gladwell. 'Jane wanted her to do it and they obviously had similar views.' The 53-minute television documentary was broadcast on Channel Four in January 1987, followed by a short season of Güney's films, and screened ten months later at the Festival dei Popoli, in Florence, Italy.

Whereas the repression experienced by Güney was internal, the countries of Indo-China, in South-east Asia, had in the 1960s and 1970s been the cockpit of a war fought by an external force, the US army. Christie opposed the United States's war in Vietnam, and in 1979 had been at the centre of a row over Michael Cimino's powerful film *The Deer Hunter*. As one of seven jurors at the 29th Berlin Film Festival, her contract forbade her from making public statements about any of the pictures being screened. This did not stop her issuing press releases in support of film-makers from the Soviet Union, Eastern Europe and Cuba who left the event in protest at the picture's depiction of the Vietcong. 'I don't believe you can portray an entire nation as sadists, then claim it has been done for dramatic effect,' said Christie, who believed this encouraged racism and war.

This came shortly after China's incursion across Vietnam's border, in February 1979, after repeated attacks on the country from

Cambodia by Pol Pot's murderous Khmer Rouge. Professor Rostislav Yurenyev, head of the Soviet delegation at the Berlin Film Festival, declared the screening of *The Deer Hunter* as particularly offensive 'at a time when Vietnam is subjected to new barbaric aggression on the part of China'. Cuba, Hungary, Czechoslovakia and East Germany followed the Soviets' lead by withdrawing from the festival.

Eight years later, Christie narrated the documentary film *Agent Orange—Policy of Poison*, about the effects of the United States's use of the deadly chemical dioxin during the Vietnam War, including the birth of blind and deformed babies for years to come.

In 1988 Christie did more than just narrate a documentary on another urgent international issue—she travelled to Cambodia to make a film for the British charity Oxfam, warning of the prospect of the genocidal Khmer Rouge regime returning to power there. After the horrors inflicted on the country by Pol Pot over four years—including possibly more than two million people murdered—the Vietnamese had overthrown the Khmer Rouge in 1979. Vietnam tried to restore normality to the Southeast Asian country, which had previously endured civil war and American bombing as an extension of the Vietnam War.

The United States and its Western allies,

including Britain, denied help to Cambodia because they refused to recognize the Vietnamese, who had defeated the Americans. China, as the West's newest trading partner, also opposed the new government and continued its support for Pol Pot, so his representative continued to take Cambodia's seat at the United Nations.

The Vietnamese were under pressure to withdraw from the country to allow the Cambodian people to govern themselves. Oxfam, which has a reputation for bringing relief to countries regardless of their politics and had operated there for almost ten years without any money from Western governments, feared the return of Pol Pot. A proposal to allow the Khmer Rouge an equal say in a new, four-part coalition government could, it warned, give them the opportunity to use its greater number of troops to take over by force. Oxfam and thirty-three other charities were behind the book *Punishing the Poor: The International Isolation of Kampuchea*, published earlier in 1988, which spelled out the reality that the relief operation in Cambodia had been more subject to political factors than any other of the twentieth century.

Christie already contributed to Oxfam, and on being asked by the charity to make the film felt that she should give any help she could. 'I am glad I agreed,' she said on her return. 'I was a voyeur; I was moved and angered by what I saw and heard; I was impressed by the survivors. The distress I feel, what has given me sleepless nights since my return, is the certainty that it could happen again—and with our tacit approval.'

While in Cambodia, Christie visited Tuol Sleng Extermination Centre, where the Khmer Rouge photographed their victims—12,000 men, women and children—before torturing and murdering them. 'There are walls and walls of photographs of faces, the faces of people who knew they were about to be tortured, who knew they were probably about to die,' explained Christie. 'When they are the faces of little children, it is more than you can bear to look at them.' The actress, who was able to speak to Cambodians in English and French, met a hydraulic engineer who, like many, had been forced to work up to eighteen hours a day in the fields under Pol Pot's regime. She also spoke to the Minister for Health, one of only seven people left in the country with medical expertise after the Khmer Rouge's purge of anyone with knowledge. Their aim was to take Cambodia back to 'Year Zero' and a 'pure' society, allowing them to restructure it from scratch in their own totalitarian mould.

A philosophy lecturer who survived those years told Christie, 'We have hope because we believe there is still reason in the world but if the Khmer Rouge come back we will know that the world has lost its reason.' Keen to ensure this message enjoyed the widest possible coverage, Christie gave an extensive interview to Brenda Polan for the *Guardian* and, two days after it was published, appeared as television chat-show host Michael Aspel's guest in *Aspel & Company*. Having long turned down requests for television interviews, Christie was quick to explain on screen that her only reason for changing that policy was to alert people to the potential horror.

In the next decade, less would be heard of Christie on one soapbox or another, but her public support for causes and concerns fitted neatly into the 1980s. Her choices of film in that time were largely influenced by a social and political awareness that had reached maturity. In between all this, Christie made a handful of more conventional films in the 1980s, as well as starring in television productions in Britain, Germany and Australia—her first small-screen acting roles for more than twenty years.

CHAPTER SIXTEEN

PICTURES, PEOPLE AND POLITICS

During the 1980s, Christie balanced her desire to act in pictures that reflected her own concerns with those that she was simply attracted to as films. After completing the apocalyptic *Memoirs of a Survivor*, Christie finally achieved her ambition to star in a French-made picture by making *Les Quarantièmes Rugissants* (*The Roaring Forties*) alongside Jacques Perrin, who had been her co-star in the abandoned *Sophie et le Capitaine*. Director Christian de Chalonge had just finished making the post-holocaust film *Malevil*, based on Robert Merle's novel about a small group in France who survive a nuclear war. So he and Christie came to *Les Quarantièmes Rugissants* with an interest in common.

For many years after reading Ron Hall and Nicholas Tomalin's book *The Last Strange Voyage of Donald Crowhurst*, it had been actor-producer Perrin's ambition to bring to the screen the story of the cheating British novice yachtsman. In 1968 Crowhurst was believed to have committed suicide after disappearing from his craft during the final lap of a non-stop, round-the-globe sailing competition

233

organized by the *Sunday Times* newspaper.

When the opportunity came, in 1981, there was financial backing totalling 29,000 francs (then about $4,142,000) from television stations in West Germany and Sierra Leone, as well as French film companies. The story was updated to 1982, the race moved to France and Crowhurst became Frenchman Julien Dantec, with Christie as his English wife, Catherine. Michel Serrault acted the yachtsman's unscrupulous press agent, Barral.

Although most of the filming was done in France, some took place in Sierra Leone, which doubled as Brazil. There the 'hero'—an electronics expert who has little experience of sailing—secretly anchors after temporarily abandoning the race. The sailing action afforded some excitement, but overall the film turned out to be a disappointment and Christie was given little scope for imposing herself on it. Even in Paris, where it was released in the summer of 1982, *Les Quarantièmes Rugissants*—running to 132 minutes and built entirely around the performance of Perrin—failed to attract cinemagoers.

In January 1983, another, more promising British picture starring Christie was released in British cinemas. Her pairing with Alan Bates for the third time on screen, in Rebecca West's First World War love story, *The Return of the Soldier*, certainly looked much happier and, with Glenda Jackson and Ann-Margret also featured, the line-up was impressive.

Bates played an English officer returning shell-shocked from the horrors of the trenches to his frivolous, aristocratic and tyrannical wife (Christie) in the class-conscious English countryside, as she copes with the fact that the hostilities have dashed her social aspirations. Bates cannot remember her but longs for an earlier love, an innkeeper's daughter from a lower class (Jackson), who is now a dowdy housewife. At the same time, the officer's repressed spinster cousin (Ann-Margret) yearns for him.

Director Alan Bridges had won the Golden Palm at the 1973 Cannes Film Festival for *The Hireling*, a screen version of another L.P. Hartley class tragedy set in the first part of the century. Ann Skinner, previously John Schlesinger's script supervisor, had read the novel of *The Return of the Soldier* with enthusiasm in 1967. She and Simon Relph, who both worked with Bridges on *The Hireling*, set up Skreba Films in 1978 with script supervisor Zelda Barron and took an option on the book. Perhaps appropriately, after his screenplays for *The Go-Between* and other upper-class period dramas, Harold Pinter was approached by Skinner to write the script, but he was busy with *The French Lieutenant's Woman*. So she and Relph went to Hugh Whitemore, who had written the film version of *All Creatures Great and Small* and contributed to the television series *Elizabeth R.* Glenda Jackson, who starred in that series, as well as the 1978 film version of Whitemore's stage play *Stevie*, was brought in after the writer started work on the script. Michael Apted was originally hired as director, but he left Britain to start a successful career in Hollywood (he directed *Agatha*, from which Christie pulled out after breaking a wrist). So Skinner and Relph turned to Bridges, who had worked with Jackson on the television play *Let's Murder Vivaldi*, before bringing Christie and Bates into the cast.

Despite having three major stars, the producers found it difficult to get financial backing for the film. They tried to show that it was marketable worldwide, a love story to which anyone could relate, but there were reservations about the fact that it was set in 1916. At the same time, it emerged that MGM had bought the rights to the book in 1920 and passed them on to Warner Brothers twenty-five years later. This problem was finally resolved, as was that of finding a backer. In February 1981, an independent investor in the United States, Los Angeles facial surgeon Barry Cooper, agreed to become executive producer and arrange finance for the film.

Another star name, the Swedish-born actress Ann-Margret, who worked with Skinner on director Richard Attenborough's

Magic, was added to the cast, and in October 1981 the formidable trio of actresses gathered for location filming in the East Sussex countryside. Firle Place, ancestral home of the late Henry Rainald, 6th Viscount Gage, provided the setting for the large house to which the soldier returns. 'I looked at the three of us standing there on the first day,' said Jackson, 'and I thought to myself, what are we doing here? You couldn't have found three more different people. It was a laugh.'

On set, tension developed between the three actresses, although this never turned into anything unpleasant. Fittingly, considering his previous film with Christie, Alan Bates acted as a go-between, ensuring that the trio did not clash, and they all went their own ways once the cameras stopped rolling. During breaks in filming, they hid themselves away in their respective trailers and, when shooting finished every day, Christie and Ann-Margret each returned to rented accommodation nearby, while Jackson drove home to south London. Scenes of the small Edwardian house where Jackson's character lived were shot in a terrace outside Nottingham that retained the character of the time, in a hamlet where miners lived.

But filming ground to a halt after several weeks' shooting when the American backer's money dried up. Cooper, who had already provided $500,000, claimed that he had failed to get cash promised him by a Canadian lawyer, J. Gordon Arnold. In the event, Arnold and Skreba worked out a rescue package in which Brent Walker Pictures would finance the rest of the production. Arnold would become executive producer, alongside Edward Simons and Brent Walker's John Quested, who had worked as an assistant director on *Young Cassidy*, one of Christie's earliest films.

Brent Walker's faith in *The Return of the Soldier* proved justified when it was selected as one of three British entries at the Cannes Film Festival, in May 1982. However, its chances were threatened when Cooper tried to get the High Court in London to issue an injunction banning the screening of the picture at Cannes without his credit as executive producer. Although the judge expressed his sympathy, he concluded that forbidding the film's screening would do more harm to the picture than to Cooper.

By then Christie had filmed most of her next picture, *Heat and Dust*, Ismail Merchant and James Ivory's colourful and mesmerizing production of Ruth Prawer Jhabvala's Booker Prize-winning novel about the British in India. For Christie, it was a return to the country of her birth and she was unsure what to expect. 'It was too far away in my memory and when I got there I found that I was amnesiac about it,' she explained. 'There's a thing called infantile

238

amnesia and I think I suffer from it. It's where simply nothing is familiar, nothing is recalled.'

But Christie's return to her roots was to provide a lasting memory. She felt free there as she filmed, going with the enquiring mind and curiosity of Anne, the character she played in the film. The picture, adapted for the screen by Jhabvala herself, was an East-meets-West story that follows Anne's trip to research the story of her great-aunt, Olivia (played by newcomer Greta Scacchi). Olivia had caused a scandal in India's British community in Satipur during the 1920s by falling in love with a nawab (prince—played by Shashi Kapoor), becoming pregnant and, after having an abortion, living the rest of her life in exile in a house built by her lover.

The mystical qualities of the great sub-continent also enmesh Anne, who falls for her Indian landlord (Zakir Hussain) but decides to keep the baby she is expecting by him, retreating to Olivia's house for the birth. Anne's search for what has become of her great-aunt is aided by Olivia's letters home to her sister and the recollections in India of Harry Hamilton-Paul (Nickolas Grace), an old English cynic, who, as the nawab's former jester and sycophant, is able to give an Indian perspective on what happened almost sixty years earlier.

The two women's stories are intercut in this evocative film, directed by Ivory, with photography by Walter Lassally, who had worked on *Memoirs of a Survivor* with Christie, and notable contributions from production designer Wilfred Shingleton, costume designer Barbara Lane and composer Richard Robbins. Other stars featured were Christopher Cazenove as Olivia's husband, the young assistant district collector Douglas Rivers, Julian Glover, Susan Fleetwood, Madhur Jaffrey and Barry Foster. Christie's narration, as Anne, holds the two parallel strands of the film together. Anne's search echoed Christie's own desire to discover her roots, both of them delving back into events that happened in British India in the early twentieth century.

Heat and Dust, financed by Rank, the Curzon Cinema, Britain's forthcoming Channel Four television company and others, was Merchant Ivory's biggest production in their twenty years of making celebrated independent films together, although its £1.1 million budget was still small by modern standards. Merchant, a Bombay-born Muslim, had teamed up with Ivory after the Irish-American filmed a documentary in India and became fascinated by the sub-continent. *Heat and Dust* was the latest in their string of pictures about the country, which included *The Householder*, *Shakespeare Wallah*, *Bombay Talkie* and *Autobiography of a Princess*.

'Because the production values were more opulent than before, it became a constant fight to find the right props and details,' said Merchant. 'Jewellery, for instance, had to be borrowed from a lady in India, and she would come in the morning with it all in a box and stay on the set all day and take it back in the evening. The thought of losing any of it was a nightmare in itself; the insurance alone was about quarter of our entire budget. Period films are so much more difficult—you have to beg, borrow or steal anything you can.'

Landing Christie was a major boon for the producer. 'It's very unusual to find such intelligent acting combined with the star personality, and Julie certainly has that,' said Merchant. 'Her commitment to this film was very encouraging and helpful and I would say that she did a lot more than her share.' Christie herself was enthusiastic about working with the director. 'I did *Heat and Dust* because I like James Ivory's work,' she explained. 'I like *Roseland*, *Autobiography of a Princess* and *Savages* all very much. It seemed a great thing to do a film with him.'

While shooting around Hyderabad with a mixed British and Indian crew, between February and April 1982, the 'unstarry' star turned down an air-conditioned room in a modern hotel and stayed at a nearby traditional Indian one. However, Christie's ecological concerns dismayed at least one of those present, director of photography Walter Lassally's agent, Kate Campbell. 'Julie

241

suggested that we must save water by not pulling the chain when we went to the toilet,' she said. 'But we were all in a modern hotel on a lake. It seemed a little foolish.'

Costume designer Barbara Lane recalled, 'Her left-wing leanings came out. I heard that she didn't flush the toilet in the Indian hotel every time she used it. She wanted desperately to be sensible and do the proper thing, but she did go to the other hotel to swim in the pool! I'm quite socialist, but I had no point of contact with Julie on that. She's very dogmatic about her beliefs and what she says is right, whatever anyone else says.'

One actor who empathized with her concerns was Nickolas Grace, a fellow graduate of both the Central School of Speech and Drama and Frinton Summer Theatre. 'We hadn't previously met each other,' he recalled, 'but Terence Stamp is a mutual friend of ours, so we got talking about him, then about Central and Frinton. She was thrilled about going back to India to do a movie and tried to do as many ethnic things as possible, such as living a more simple life in what was like an old English Raj hotel, where you couldn't have a shower. She wanted to get back to her Indian roots and, once she realized that I was the kind of guy who wanted to know more about the natives, we went to the market together in Hyderabad, shopping for cheap silk and cotton.'

On set, all the signs of British colonialism in the 1920s were captured to perfection, with the women's parasols and petticoats and the men's brandy and cigars providing detail that captured the atmosphere of the period. Barbara Lane had just two days to find or create Christie's clothes because the modern-day scenes were shot first, shortly after the cast and crew arrived in Hyderabad. A frantic time was spent touring local markets and sewing costumes through the night.

Walter Lassally's photography helped to reflect the different moods of the film. The subtle, softened colours that he achieved were something he had perfected twenty years earlier while filming *Tom Jones*, using a fine silk net over the camera lens. For *Heat and Dust*, Lassally and director Ivory decided to differentiate the 1923 and 1982 scenes with 'a combination of the art direction, the lighting and the camera movement', explained the director of photography, 'so that the modern sequences are somewhat more strident in both colour and movement, whilst the 1923 scenes are more gentle and more pastel.'

But filming almost ground to a halt when finance ran out before the last Hyderabad sequences, featuring Greta Scacchi and Christopher Cazenove, were shot. Barbara Lane had no money to buy costumes and the caterers refused to supply food until they were paid. 'Christopher and Greta found the money to pay the poor Indian caterers and we all put in whatever we had to get some costumes I needed,' said Lane. Shashi Kapoor took care of the cast and crew's hotel bills.

Then the whole entourage flew to Srinigar, in the Himalayas, for the final scenes, in which Christie is seen as Anne visiting Olivia's mountain retreat in anticipation of her own baby's birth. They were leaving an unusual heatwave in Hyderabad for snow in the mountains. As they boarded a plane in Delhi, Christie fumed with anger at having to hand over an item of her hand baggage to security people. Barbara Lane recalled:

She had a Swiss Army knife and they took it off her. She was really angry and said, 'Do you know who you're talking to?' It was so out of character, but she said she had carried the knife all over the world and needed it for the trek she was planning into the Himalayas once filming had finished. So, when one of the crew members came up to her during the flight and asked if she wanted to go to the front of the plane and see the landing, because it's very spectacular, she said, 'No, because they took my knife and I don't want to speak to anybody to do with this airline.'

With the Indian filming over, Christie trekked into the Himalayas with boyfriend

Duncan Campbell on a journey of rediscovery in the land of her birth. Soon, however, she had to return to London to shoot the picture's first scene, of Anne with Harry Hamilton-Paul (Nickolas Grace) before her own visit of discovery, in August 1982.

Two days' filming was planned in the beautiful garden of a Hampstead house owned by the publisher John Murray, whose company originally published the books of Lord Byron and Jane Austen. A dispute over Grace's contract displayed for him how loyal Christie was to her friends, even to one so new. 'Julie is always incredibly supportive and stands by other actors,' he said. 'Merchant Ivory said they wanted me to do two days' shooting in London, but I was on stage every night playing Mozart in *Amadeus* and pointed out that it would be tricky to fit it in. They said I was under contract, although I thought it was outside the contract I had signed and my agent couldn't find the top copy. Equity, the actors' union, said they would stand by me and Julie said, "If you're sure you never signed the top copy, I won't shoot it. I'll stick with you." In the end, Equity advised me that it would be best for my career to go ahead with it. As we were shooting, Julie kept joking, "We can stop any time and walk out!"' Grace took little persuading when Christie later asked him to join her on a speakers' platform at the time London was declared a Nuclear-Free Zone.

On its release in Britain in January 1983, *Heat and Dust*—Merchant Ivory's tenth picture to be written by Jhabvala—was widely praised. David Robinson noted in *The Times* that Christie was 'notably more at ease as Anne, the girl of 1982, than in other recent film roles'. In the *New York Times*, Vincent Canby wrote, 'Miss Christie, who makes too few movies, is lovely and commonsensical as Anne. Her intelligence perfectly reflects that of the film itself.'

Heat and Dust opened the doors for Merchant Ivory Productions to make more widely screened films, such as *A Room with a View*, *Maurice*, *Howards End* and *The Remains of the Day*. For Christie, it was a rewarding experience. 'I probably made more friends in my time in India than I've ever made anywhere in such a short time,' she enthused. 'Certainly more than I made in England in such a short time. I found the women magnificent and the people very courageous. I was moved by them as you are with people you care about—but I think their government is absolutely appalling.'

More fond memories were brought back when Christie teamed up with director John Schlesinger and Alan Bates yet again, in a television film version of Terence Rattigan's classic 1950s double-bill play *Separate Tables*, produced jointly by HTV of Britain and Primetime Television of America. The lead roles had originally been taken on stage by

Margaret Leighton and Eric Porter.

This presented Christie with the opportunity to act the two roles of the bitchy ex-wife of a Labour junior minister whose career has been ruined by drink (Bates), and a frumpy, mother-dominated spinster who falls for a bogus retired major (Bates again) bound over on a charge of insulting behaviour.

'I remember *Separate Tables* in 1954 as a thoroughly good evening in the theatre and now there is the absolute delight of working again with Alan and Julie for the first time since we did *Far from the Madding Crowd* 17 years ago,' said Schlesinger, who found no discernible change in the actress. 'She is no harder to direct these days,' he added. 'She is more experienced and more sure, no question, and she has a magic which is indefinable, but she is just as malleable, just as co-operative, just as professional—and works just as hard.'

However, Christie originally had doubts about appearing in this pair of one-act plays, *Table by the Window* and *Table Number Seven*. 'I thought, "Do I really want to do this extraordinary material?"' she explained. 'But I decided to accept because I really wanted to work with John and Alan again.' Claire Bloom joined the pair in both plays, acting the hotel manager.

Rehearsals were done at a hall in Hammersmith, west London, before the play was recorded at HTV's Bristol studios in front of an audience. Schlesinger found that he could still be surprised by Christie, especially in her role as Sybil, the dowdy spinster. 'We used disfiguring make-up,' he explained. 'I added protruding teeth and odd things to her nose to make her look as if she had always worn glasses. But she lived the role of Sybil so completely I almost didn't recognize her at first. It was a measure of how much she'd matured since I last worked with her.' A multi-room set was designed for the production and Schlesinger approached it as a television play, not simply as a piece of theatre being recorded for the screen.

Separate Tables was screened on American television in March 1983 and on ITV in Britain the following January. On its transmission in America, in the early days of the pay-TV channel HBO, John J. O'Connor wrote in the *New York Times*, 'Miss Christie and Mr Bates are superb—she cold and drawn as the model, dowdy and trembling as the daughter; he puffy and belligerent as the failed politician, blimpish and pathetic as the fraud . . . Rattigan and his reputation have been well served.' The trade paper the *Hollywood Reporter* remarked on the unusually high standard of production and performances for a programme shown on pay-TV, noting, 'Bates and Christie both display impressive range and versatility, along with intense credibility.'

A planned reunion with director Robert

248

Altman for his adaptation of Ernest Hemingway's novel *Across the River and into the Trees* failed to happen when the project fell through, in 1985. Christie had been set to star with Roy Scheider, best known for his performances in *The French Connection* and *Jaws*.

But she remained in famous company when she travelled to New York to make *Power*, which gave her the opportunity to work with legendary American director Sidney Lumet and heart-throb actor Richard Gere for the first time. She played the British investigative reporter and ex-wife of Gere, who acted an unprincipled media consultant in this satire on the packaging of politics. The Hollywood star saw *Power* as more challenging than his previous roles. Gene Hackman was also featured, as Gere's former mentor and partner, along with Kate Capshaw, as his girlfriend and right-hand woman, and E.G. Marshall, as his one-time political idol.

Lumet, who emerged as one of the new wave of directors in the 1950s, had made his name with films such as *Serpico*, *Dog Day Afternoon* and *Network*, a satire that had already explored the lengths to which television companies will go to attract big audiences in the ratings wars. Unfortunately, *Power* failed to live up to that picture or the strengths of its leading man and lady. 'Sidney and I had wanted to work together for a long

249

time,' said Christie, 'and the story was, is, intriguing, though I don't think it quite zings off.'

However, she pointed out, 'Sidney's a wonderful person to work with. With *Power*, he rehearsed us for two weeks before starting shooting. So for once we knew how things fitted together.' Christie had never previously worked with Gere, who starred in *American Gigolo*—which she had rejected—and became box-office dynamite with *An Officer and a Gentleman*. 'I hadn't seen any of his movies, so I didn't know anything about him, except that he was meant to be very sexy and attractive,' she said. 'He's that, but also he's a really good actor.'

Power was not to do much for the careers of either Gere or Christie, with Victoria Mather in *The Times* contending that it was 'much like a television series pretending to be important'. *Variety* pointed out that it had 'little appeal to teens and questionable prospects among adults at a time when polls show overwhelming popular satisfaction with the most tube-savvy President ever' [Ronald Reagan]. The best reviews were reserved for Hackman.

During filming Christie stayed with an old friend, production designer Tony Walton, and his wife in an old apartment block off Broadway. The picture gave her the opportunity to form a bond with Gere, who also yearned to have a private life away from

250

the fame of his public one and had already developed an interest in China's human rights abuses in Tibet. The pair had long discussions during which Christie, heavily involved in campaigning against the United States's support for the Contras in Nicaragua at the time, urged Gere to go to Central America. This led him, after filming, to become a dedicated campaigner for justice in Nicaragua, Honduras and El Salvador. His efforts, like those of Christie in pursuit of her humanitarian objectives, were untiring and soon seen to be genuine.

Gere also appeared on Dick Cavett's American chat-show, agreeing to talk about his films for ten minutes as long as the rest of the hour-long programme could be devoted to talking about a three-week fact-finding mission to Central America. He accompanied Vietnam veteran Charlie Clemens, an American doctor, and collected testimonies from the victims of terror in the region. Two years later Christie made a similar appearance on Michael Aspel's British chat-show so that she could highlight the threat still facing Cambodia.

Christie's next destinations, after filming *Power*, were Argentina, to shoot *Miss Mary*, and Tunisia, for the filming of *La Mémoire Tatouée*. But for the rest of the 1980s she took another long break from the big screen. Her only performances were on television, in two mini-series. First she teamed up with Burt Lancaster in *Vater and Sohne (Fathers and Sons)*, the tale of a German chemical industry family and their collaboration with the Nazi government. In the German programme, she played Charlotte Deutz, who is blackmailed by her lover into giving him control of her company shares.

Then Christie travelled to Australia, in March 1988, to make *Dadah Is Death* (dadah meaning drug-trafficking in Malay; the programme was shown in some countries as *A Long Way from Home*). This was the true story of a British mother's unsuccessful fight to save her son from the gallows in Malaysia for smuggling heroin. Christie played Barbara Barlow, whose 27-year-old son Kevin had been hanged two years earlier despite her attempts to get his death sentence commuted, claiming that he had been framed by international drug barons.

The Barlows had emigrated from Britain to Australia in the 1960s and failed to find the Brave New World which they had been seeking. They ended up living in a caravan and found no success in starting their own business. In July 1986 Kevin Barlow was hanged along with an Australian also accused of drug smuggling.

Christie had become interested in the case through her work with the UK Council for Welfare of Prisoners Abroad, and while making the mini-series in Australia and Malaysia she formed a close bond with the real Barbara Barlow, who acted as an adviser. This was another cause, and Christie became passionate about it. She said:

People don't want to diagnose the problem of drug-trafficking. They just say, 'Kill them.' Everybody wants vengeance. Compassion has gone out of fashion. Barlow was the product of a society which has been declining for a long time . . . There's a complete irrationality about the drugs issue when you look at all the people who are dying through alcohol and cigarettes. Are they going to put the off-licence merchants and the cigarette companies on trial and demand the death sentence for them? Of course not.

However, Christie's enthusiasm was not given good service by the belaboured, four-hour mini-series. Also, in portraying Barbara Barlow's single-minded determination and overprotective nature, Christie was unable to generate much sympathy for her character. Similarly, Kevin Barlow (actor John Polson) was depicted as being unrepentant and only sorry that he had not been more careful.

Filming on the other side of the world, and staying in a Sydney hotel, meant that Christie had to send her regrets to David Lean that she

253

was unable to attend an eightieth birthday party in his honour, on 25 March. After finishing filming *Dadah Is Death*, Christie moved on to Cambodia to make her film for Oxfam. A return to the cinema screen was still some time away.

CHAPTER SEVENTEEN

IRISH EYES

When Christie accepted a matriarchal role in *Fools of Fortune*, the tale of an Anglo-Irish family's disintegration during the war of independence fought in the early twentieth century, it might have been seen as a willingness to work back in the film world's mainstream. However, apart from the made-for-television movie *The Railway Station Man*, also set in Ireland, it was her only film released during the first half of the 1990s, although both productions were happy experiences for the actress.

After campaigning for human rights in far-flung corners of the world, Christie looked closely at historical events in Ireland for the first time. 'I make it my business to keep informed about international affairs,' she explained, 'but I was appalled about how little I knew about this place that my country had been so intimately involved with over the years, a place just across the water. The English suffer from an ignorance of Ireland, and I think it's probably orchestrated that way because people are always kept in ignorance of their so-called enemies. British involvement goes back to the 18th century, when the Irish language and traditions were all repressed.' In fact, England's conquest of Ireland had started in the twelfth century with Henry II's invasion. The roots of native Catholic resentment took hold with Oliver Cromwell's land confiscation 500 years later.

Fools of Fortune, a 1983 Whitbread Prize-winning novel by William Trevor, focused on one family living in rural Ireland in one of the most cataclysmic periods of the country's history. The 1916 Easter Rising, when Catholics declared the existence of an independent Irish Republic, had been put down by the British, but the execution of some of the leaders caused public opinion in Ireland to move in their favour. The call for independence would not go away, and in 1920 war broke out. The Royal Irish Constabulary, which was seen as propping up the British establishment, was supplemented by auxiliary police units recruited from across the water, mainly from those who had fought in the First World War. They became known for lootings, burnings and massacres, and were called the 'Black and Tans' because of their clothing—a

255

mix of khaki army uniforms and dark-green police belts and hats.

The murder of one of the Quinton family's workers by a Republican, on suspicion of spying for the British forces, and the Black and Tans' burning down of their home and murder of Mr Quinton and two of his three children formed the starting point for *Fools of Fortune*. Michael Kitchen played Christie's doomed husband, with up-and-coming Scottish actor Iain Glen cast as her surviving son, Willie (although the character was portrayed as a child by Sean T McClory). Niamh Cusack, of the legendary Irish acting family, took the role of their maid, Josephine.

The horrific events lead Willie to become withdrawn and introspective, and his mother to become a manic depressive who finds solace in the bottle. When Mrs Quinton commits suicide, Willie is comforted by his childhood friend Marianne, played by American actress Mary Elizabeth Mastrantonio. Later, the couple are parted and Marianne returns after giving birth to a baby daughter, only to discover that Willie has murdered the leader of the Black and Tans and gone into exile on an island off Wales. Mother and child stay with his aunts in the only surviving part of the ravaged Quinton house, until the dying maid calls Willie home, where he is reunited with Marianne and the daughter he has never known. This love story was the film's central theme, with the historical events as a backdrop, and Christie's star billing came below those of Mastrantonio and Glen.

In fact director Joseph Losey and writer Harold Pinter had previously planned to make a screen version of *Fools of Fortune* and took an option on the book even before it won the Whitbread Prize. However, they had difficulty finding financial backing and were unable to resolve that before Losey's death, in 1984.

In that year, Tim Bevan and Sarah Radclyffe formed a new British production company, Working Title, which became noted for films such as *My Beautiful Laundrette*, *Personal Services*, *Wish You Were Here* and *A World Apart*. They acquired the screen rights to *Fools of Fortune* in 1987, hired Michael Hirst to write the screenplay and decided that the perfect director would be Pat O'Connor. He had had experience of making documentaries with the country's television network, RTE, before directing films such as the celebrated *Cal*, featuring Helen Mirren and John Lynch, and *A Month in the Country*. He had also collaborated with Trevor on a television version of his book *The Ballroom of Romance*. The jigsaw was completed when Bevan and Radclyffe put together an international cast, combining Irish actors with Christie, Iain Glen and Michael Kitchen from Britain, and Mary Elizabeth Mastrantonio from the United States.

After three years away from film sets, Christie was enthusiastic about acting in *Fools of Fortune*. 'There are some things you just cannot refuse,' she said. 'It had a great script from a wonderful book and I thought Pat O'Connor's *Cal* was excellent. Also, I thought what it was saying was valuable. Mrs Quinton is a very politicized woman, the English wife of an Irishman, and I think that what is interesting about the film is that it blurs the rigid lines in people's minds about who stands for what and why.'

During three months' shooting in the Irish Republic during the summer of 1989, Christie threw herself into the role, transforming Mrs Quinton from a quiet mother living an idyllic life in the Irish countryside to a tormented woman unable to cope with the loss of most of her family. 'This is someone who has spent her life fighting for justice, an optimist, yet the loss of everything she holds dear destroys her faith and she loses her grasp and can only rail against the fates in a completely useless way,' explained Christie. 'You never know why a person goes over the edge but I tried to portray what happens when all hope is lost.'

While filming in the market town of Mullingar and the Irish republic's capital, Dublin, production designer Jamie Leonard was struck by Christie's down-to-earth nature. 'She was incredibly easy to work with and without arrogance, which is rare,' he recalled.

'Julie had a professional detachment and didn't feel that she had to make her mark among the crew or prove herself in any way. Having been out of films for quite a while and living in Wales, she had a tranquillity that was there until she needed to prove otherwise in her performance. On the surface she was quite delicate, but underneath she was robust.'

Mrs Quinton proved to be Christie's most effective screen role since *Heat and Dust*, which had also successfully combined strong drama with historical events. The Irish landscape and atmospheric music helped to make *Fools of Fortune* a worthy addition to Christie's list of credits, although the film made little impact at the box office. Significantly, the picture signalled that the sex symbol of the Swinging Sixties, who was fifty several months before its release, was happy to have moved on to playing characters of her own age and no longer automatically enjoyed top billing. 'I've started to get a lot of vulnerable mothers,' she said, 'as well as women not unlike myself—middle-aged, whatever I am, strong, active.'

After another break from filming, Christie returned to Ireland in the spring of 1991 to be reunited with Donald Sutherland in *The Railway Station Man*, Shelagh Delaney's screen adaptation of Jennifer Johnston's novel. The historical backdrop to this Irish thriller was the modern-day Troubles, with Christie playing the widowed mother who moves to a remote, coastal village and takes up painting after her husband is mistakenly killed in an ambush. Sutherland arrives as a maimed American veteran of the Korean War who loves trains and sets about restoring a disused station. Both running away from their past, Helen Cuffe and Roger Hawthorne are drawn together, and film enthusiasts eagerly anticipated the reunion of Christie and Sutherland almost twenty years after their passionate partnership in *'Don't Look Now'*.

As in that film, the pair played two people rebuilding their lives after tragedy, and *The Railway Station Man* does feature a love scene between the couple, but director Michael Whyte wisely opted not to make it as overtly erotic as the one they had previously shared on screen. In fact, the middle-aged lovers are interrupted by Helen's son, Jack (Frank MacCusker), who becomes involved with the IRA. Further tragedy follows when Roger crashes into a truck filled with IRA explosives, and Helen once again picks up the pieces of her life.

This was one of Whyte's first films, after a background in television that included making the award-winning documentary *Creggan*, about a Londonderry Catholic community living through the Troubles in Northern Ireland. *The Railway Station Man* was made specially for television, with Turner Pictures of

America providing two-thirds of the £2.5 million budget and BBC Films of Britain the rest.

Roger Randall-Cutler, who had just produced *The Commitments* in Ireland, was approached with the idea of turning *The Railway Station Man* into a film by American producer Lauren Joy Sand. He read the book, was enthusiastic and immediately thought that Shelagh Delaney, who had written the script for another of his films, *Dance with a Stranger*, would be ideal as the screenwriter and Christie for the lead role of Helen.

In casting Canadian Sutherland as the Korean War veteran—originally an English Second World War veteran in the book—Randall-Cutler was able to satisfy the American co-producers. 'We also had to get together someone with Julie where there was a chemistry, not necessarily the same chemistry as in *'Don't Look Now'*, and I saw the marketing possibilities,' he explained. 'I felt that using Donald didn't damage Jennifer Johnston's novel at all. He could just as easily be an American who had this obsession with railways and trains.'

Filming took place over seven weeks in Donegal, the northernmost county of the Irish Republic, during April and May 1991. Much of the shooting was done in and around a cliffside cottage at Glencolumbkille, which was Helen's house in the story, with the wild Atlantic on one side and the rugged Donegal hills on the other. The railway station scenes were shot in Gweedore. Off set, Christie and Sutherland went their separate ways, she a short distance to a white-washed seaside cottage, he an hour's drive to a hotel outside Donegal town. But, on set, they relished the opportunity to reignite the flames of two decades earlier.

'There was a great chemistry between us in *'Don't Look Now'*, and it came across on the screen very well,' said Christie. 'We seem to have the same chemistry today. I wanted to work with Donald again. I like him and trust him. What we share in the film certainly rekindled memories.'

However, producer Roger Randall-Cutler recalled the concern of director Michael Whyte and Irish actor John Lynch over a scene in which Helen Cuffe swims naked in the sea, comes out and walks along the beach towards Damian Sweeney, played by Lynch, even though Christie had agreed to do it. Randall-Cutler said:

Everyone knew how cold it was. So I put that scene as late as possible in the schedule because we knew that the weather would improve over the course of the shoot, although the temperature of the water would not. I moved it further back in the schedule several times in what was graphically becoming an obsession by the

262

actor and the director, who became increasingly angst-ridden on behalf of Julie about the prospect of doing this scene. This became more and more vocal and a bone of contention between them and me, to the point where I decided to reassure them that Julie was happy to do the scene. But I went to see Julie in her cottage and told her that I would be prepared to go in the water before she did it to establish that it was possible to do the scene. She said, no, it was perfectly OK. 'I'm happy to do the scene,' she told me. 'I don't know what all the fuss is about.'

The day came to film and it was quite bright and sunny, although it was cold. We had every possible facility for her standing by to resuscitate Julie as soon as she came out of the water, such as heaters, a tent, towels and dressing gowns. We also had a stunt double to do the long shots, both running into the water and a lot of the swimming. But, as soon as we came in on the mid- or close-up shots and where Julie had to walk out of the water, it was important that it was Julie herself and she had nothing on. We established that it would be done in the best possible taste and filmed from behind her.

We came to shoot the scene and Julie simply did it, as required. I enjoyed the fact that Julie, by her action, had shown not only extraordinary commitment and professionalism to the work in hand. It demonstrated that the woman had shown up the alarming and strange behaviour of the actor and director.

The Railway Station Man received its premiere at the Madrid Film Festival in April 1992 but did not appear on British television, in BBC2's 'Screen Two' slot, until December 1993. Like *Fools of Fortune*, it made no great waves but did no harm at all to Christie and was a satisfying experience for her.

At about this time, more sadness came into Christie's life with the news of former fiancé Don Bessant's death. He had slipped quietly out of the spotlight when she spent more time in the United States and became very publicly associated with Warren Beatty. In 1972 Bessant had left Maidstone College of Art to teach at Wolverhampton Polytechnic, although he continued to live in London. Despite suffering from throat cancer during his final year, Bessant actually died of a severe heart attack in February 1993, as his father had done little more than twenty-five years earlier. Christie was out of the country, so she was unable to attend the funeral. Aged fifty-one, Bessant had never married. 'Don was still friendly with Julie right to the end,' revealed his mother, Betty. 'I still hear from her occasionally. We are very good friends.'

Although not seen in films again during the first half of the 1990s, Christie enjoyed her first experiences of working in radio, acting in a BBC World Service production of Chekhov's *The Three Sisters* in 1990 and reading Fay Weldon short stories on BBC Radio 4 three years later, first for *Book at Bedtime*, then *Birthday!*, in two parts under its own title. She described working in the medium as 'like making love to the mike'.

Christie also increasingly loaned her voice to television, although at her home in Wales she did not have a set, preferring to listen to radio. In 1992 she narrated the moving story of *Katie and Eilish: Siamese Twins* in ITV's 'First Tuesday' documentary slot. Yorkshire Television's cameras spent a year in the Irish town of Donadea, County Kildare, following the progress of twins who were joined from the shoulder to the hip and shared a pelvis and two legs. Their parents, Liam and Mary Holton, were seen making the heartbreaking decision to separate Katie and Eilish, knowing that surgery could either help or kill them. In the event, three-year-old Eilish survived the operation at Great Ormond Street Hospital, London, but Katie died.

Among widespread critical praise for the programme, Allison Pearson of the

Independent noted: 'Julie Christie did the voiceover, but I only realized that as the credits rolled, which is the best time to notice who the narrator is. There had been no gush, no poignant pause. Matter-of-fact for matter-a-lot.'

When the programme-makers returned to the Holton family three years later to assess the surviving twin's development in *Eilish: Life Without Katie*, shown in ITV's 'Network First' strand, Christie again narrated. She did work in the same vein, for another Yorkshire Television documentary, *Small Miracles*. The film followed two sets of parents as they put their faith in a pioneering doctor at King's College Hospital, London, in the hope of saving their unborn children. The first couple had to decide whether to allow him to perform intricate laser surgery inside the mother's womb to increase the chances of their unborn twins surviving. The second mother had a rare condition in which her immune system was destroying her baby's platelets, which could cause it to bleed to death. The couple, therefore, visited the doctor weekly from their home in Cornwall so that he could transfuse platelets into the baby through the umbilical cord in order to replace those being lost.

Also seen contributing on-screen to some programmes, Christie was an obvious interviewee for director Richard Lester's 1993 BBC2 series *Hollywood UK: British Cinema in the 60s*, a fond, nostalgic reflection on that last great era of filmmaking in Britain. Lester had not been involved in the filmed interviews but was asked to present the series. 'The interview with Julie was done long before I was ever involved,' said Lester. Five years later, Christie reminisced about another great director with whom she had worked in *François Truffaut: The Man Who Loved Cinema*, and she talked about some of her favourite films in both BBC2's *Close Up* and the Channel Four series *Kiss Kiss Bang Bang*. Her continuing love of watching films had also led her, in 1990, to accept an invitation to become patron of the Welsh International Film Festival.

Christie's other interests, in justice and repression around the world, continued and in 1992 she took the opportunity to present a five-minute programme in BBC2's *Prisoners of Conscience* series, highlighting the cases of people jailed for their political beliefs. She spoke about Francisco Branco, an Indonesian father-of-eight who was imprisoned for belonging to a secret, anti-government organization. 'I said I was particularly interested in East Timor, Indonesia, because it has received such little coverage,' expained Christie. 'There were terrible massacres there in 1991 during a peaceful protest in a cemetery . . . I wouldn't do anything if I had my way but I do emerge. I've got to, if I feel very strongly about something—and I feel very strongly about the situation in East Timor.'

The actress had also previously felt very strongly about not returning to theatrical work. In the mid 1980s, she announced that she had given up the stage. 'It's too hard, and I finally said to myself that I don't have the courage to face all those people during a performance,' she said. 'Being with a large public is very difficult for me. I don't know what it would take to get me to do theatre again.'

But in 1995 she did so, acting in the West End for the first time, apart from her Royal Shakespeare Company appearances at the Aldwych thirty-one years earlier. The play was a revival of *Old Times*, Harold Pinter's enduring classic first performed in 1971, shortly after Christie had acted in his film adaptation of *The Go-Between*. Then it starred Dorothy Tutin, Colin Blakely and Vivien Merchant. This new version, directed by Christie's Australian friend Lindy Davies, was a Theatr Clwyd production that ran for four weeks in Mold, North Wales, before moving into the West End at Wyndham's Theatre in July 1995.

Davies had acted as Christie's 'performance consultant' for *Fools of Fortune*, *The Railway Station Man* and *Dragonheart*. On being approached by Helena Kaut-Howson of Theatr Clwyd, Christie agreed to play the lead role of Kate in *Old Times* on the condition that

Davies was hired as director. The character was a dreamer, suffering from memory lapses, and had withdrawn from society—Christie shared much with her.

She was joined on stage by Leigh Lawson as her husband, Deeley, and Harriet Walter as her long-lost friend, Anna; the three characters recall the joys of 1950s London after the years of post-war austerity. The triangular relationship is explored as Deeley and Anna argue over their distorted memories of Kate.

The lengthy pauses in dialogue for which Pinter's plays are noted had something in common with Christie's 'naturalistic' way of delivering lines, although it was a device that often infuriated critics. Jack Tinker of the *Daily Mail* contended that 'all the arch staccato speech patterns and the extended pauses' were saved only by the 'individual charisma' of the actors and he found Christie's 'cat-with-cream smile infinitely beguiling'. Reviews for the production and Christie were mixed. The *Independent*'s Robert Hanks insisted that 'the fixed smile is rather too cheesy and immobile, her gestures and changes of expression feel too drilled'. However, Benedict Nightingale wrote in *The Times*, 'I have seen Dorothy Tutin and Nicola Pagett play the role in London, and Marsha Mason bring a wonderful languor to it in New York; but I don't think any of them bettered Julie Christie . . . Christie fits Pinter's specifications, and in the most natural, unaffected way. This smiling English rose makes what can be a waftily erotic fantasy-figure human and real.'

During her run in *Old Times*, Christie had a moving backstage reunion with old flame Terence Stamp, who arrived with Christie's *Heat and Dust* co-star Nickolas Grace. 'We went to her dressing room and had a long gossip,' recalled Grace. 'I don't think she'd seen Terence for years and years and years, and it was clearly quite an emotional time for both of them.' Another backstage visitor was Betty Bessant, mother of Christie's long-time love Don, who had died little more than two years earlier.

The experience of acting on stage again was clearly not too arduous for Christie, nor the critical reaction too mixed, because two years later she accepted the chance to star in Vietnam-born French dramatist Marguerite Duras's 1968 play *Suzanna Andler* at the Minerva Studio, Chichester. Again directed by Lindy Davies, Christie took the title role of a desperately unhappy woman married to an unfaithful husband, finally embarking on her own affair. Looking over a Saint-Tropez house with a view to renting it for the summer, she is accompanied by her journalist lover and, during the course of the day, encounters one of her husband's mistresses. It is the story of the self-inflicted agonies of the super-rich.

But the critics were not so kind this time. Michael Billington of the *Guardian* declared that Christie lacked the 'emotional firepower' of Eileen Atkins and Susan Hampshire, whom he had previously seen in the role. He added, 'For much of the evening, Christie radiates a very English, district nurse common sense that made me feel she would have sorted out the villa business and her emotional problems in no time at all.'

Christie conceded:

The reviews weren't good, but that doesn't bother me. The only thing I don't like is malice. It sends me into a flat tail-spin. It's par for the course nowadays because prying into people's lives is how newspapers make money. It's a *sine qua non* for human freedom that we have privacy. If that's taken away we go mad. 'Celebrity' has become a public recourse and I see it as punishment for entertaining people and making them happy. I've been punished quite enough and I can't take any more.

During the stage run of *Suzanna Andler*, Christie voiced reservations about having agreed to take the role. 'The play is something I shouldn't have done,' she said. 'I went through too much agony. Even now, the lines go popping out of my head all the time and I can't rely on myself. So it's perilous. I can see how other people learn lines, but I haven't got that mind . . . I didn't see when I read it that this woman is on stage talking all the time. I didn't see that the language was almost impossible. It was like a Chinese puzzle with all the tenses muddled up.' However, Christie did show herself willing to continue entertaining and, in the second half of the 1990s, made her screen comeback.

CHAPTER EIGHTEEN

RETURN TO THE FOLD

Christie's return to the screen came with roles in a historic television serial and a special-effects-filled film. Although *Dragonheart* was shot first, the picture's elaborate computerized effects meant that it was not released until just after *Karaoke*, one of Dennis Potter's last two plays for television, written as companion pieces that, uniquely, were each shown by BBC1 and Channel Four on consecutive nights.

Potter's dying wish, expressed in a memorable, final television interview with Melvyn Bragg, was that *Karaoke* and its sequel, *Cold Lazarus*, should be screened by both channels. He successfully battled to finish the plays before his death, in June 1994, and his own production company, Whistling Gypsy, started filming the four-part *Karaoke* in London in February 1995, once agreement was reached with the BBC and Channel Four. The autobiographical drama featured Albert Finney as a television writer who discovers that he is dying of cancer, sees his latest script coming alive around him and becomes obsessed with a young nightclub hostess (played by Saffron Burrows). Christie, who appeared in two of the episodes, acted the wealthy Lady Ruth Balmer, wife of ambitious director Nick Balmer (Richard E. Grant), who cheats on her with his leading lady.

In one scene, after being beaten up, the director fervently kisses his wife in the back of a Rolls-Royce and admits his infidelity. Richard E. Grant, jotting down his regular 'Arts Diary' in the *Observer* Review section, also confessed at the time of filming that Christie had been a heroine of his since childhood. He added, 'Screen kissing with her, albeit with cotton-wool plugged inside my upper lip to simulate bruising, is something I've never imagined actually doing. I fanned my way through her greatest hits to her bemusement—"How do you remember all this stuff?" I realize with embarrassment that fan talk is a conversational cul-de-sac. I ignore it pronto, lest I dribble through the day in a state of film buff-oonery.'

The cast also included Anna Chancellor,

Hywel Bennett, Roy Hudd, Keeley Hawes, Liz Smith, Alison Steadman and Ian McDiarmid. When *Karaoke* was screened in the spring of 1996, it received mixed reviews and a disappointing average audience of only 3.37 million on BBC1 and fewer on Channel Four. *Cold Lazarus*, each episode of which was screened by Channel Four first and then repeated on BBC1 the next night, followed on immediately from *Karaoke*. However, Christie did not appear in the sequel, which was set in 2368 and told of scientists accessing the memory of Albert Finney's *Karaoke* character, whose dead body had been frozen almost 400 years earlier.

Shortly afterwards, Christie was seen in the American film *Dragonheart*, which starred Dennis Quaid as a heroic dragonslayer, the knight Bowen, who teams up with the last dragon on Earth to defeat tyrannical King Einon (David Thewlis) in tenth-century Europe. The fable was directed by Rob Cohen and shot entirely in Slovakia over five-and-a-half months in 1994, but it took another eighteen months to reach cinema screens because of the extensive editing required to add computer-generated images of the dragon, which was called Draco and voiced by Sean Connery.

It was certainly a special-effects extravaganza, costing more than $50 million, but the technical wizardry failed to make up for the picture's basic lack of substance. Patrick Swayze, Harrison Ford and Mel Gibson were all reported to have turned down the lead role, and Christie was certainly under-used as Einon's mother, Queen Aislinn, who is betrayed by her son. However, the actress enthused for the film's publicity handout, 'I felt as though I was in the middle of a fairy tale! With the glorious costumes and the castles coming out of the tops of flaming autumn forests, it was just heaven—and terrific fun.'

In any event, the sets and costumes were painstakingly created. Cast and crew filmed around the Slovakian capital of Bratislava, amid mountains, forests and Roman castles. A modern, state-of-the-art film studio in the city's Slovensky Film Studio Koliba, was used to shoot interiors, including Aislinn's bed chamber. It also became the base for the costume designers and their team, who hand-made the stars' tenth-century outfits. These were based on photographs of the Bayeux Tapestry, depicting the Norman conquest of England.

The film itself was a mix of Arthurian legend, Robin Hood, Don Quixote and *Braveheart*. Director Cohen had previously made *Dragon: The Bruce Lee Story*, an action film about the martial-arts star who died at the age of thirty-three, and he was the veteran of many episodes of the American police series

Miami Vice. Now acknowledging that the violence in that and other television programmes might have had an adverse effect on society, Cohen was determined to keep it to a minimum in *Dragonheart*, a principle that was clearly slightly at odds with the story.

The murder of Christie's character by her son was not even seen on screen because the decision was made to shoot it in shadow. 'She was such a nice character, people wouldn't want to see her die,' explained stunt co-ordinator Paul Weston, 'so you just saw her go up some stairs into darkness and obviously going to be killed.'

Christie was influenced in her decision to act in *Dragonheart* by the presence of rising British star David Thewlis, who shared the same agent, ICM. Director Cohen said:

Julie loves David, so she took his opinion very seriously. I think one of her concerns was that she didn't know anything about me. So one Sunday morning the phone rang and there was this unmistakable voice on the other end of the line. Julie and I spoke for some time, and at the end of the conversation she agreed to do the movie. I was thrilled to be working with her. I considered it to be a great honour. She always radiates this quality of vulnerability combined with intelligence. I knew she would make Aislinn a wonderful, complex character.

Producer Raffaella de Laurentiis, previously responsible for films such as *Dune* and *Conan the Destroyer*, recalled of a conversation with Christie, 'I asked her at one point why she decided to do *this* movie, after turning down so many others. She said, "Because it is a fairy tale about good and evil—and the world needs to see this." '

On set, Christie proved to be a parent figure both in and out of character. 'She was a delight to work with and mothered everyone,' said stunt co-ordinator Paul Weston. 'The weather was getting cold in Slovakia. If anyone had a cold or a sniffle, she looked after them and made sure they had medicine or whatever.'

Whatever the merits of *Dragonheart*, Christie appeared to have a new enthusiasm for the cinema. Shortly afterwards, while acting on the West End stage in *Old Times*, she accepted an invitation from British film's golden boy, actor-director Kenneth Branagh, to appear in his mammoth, four-hour screen version of *Hamlet*, using Shakespeare's entire, unedited text. Again, Christie was playing a queen, this time Hamlet's mother, Gertrude, who marries his villainous uncle, Claudius (Derek Jacobi), little more than a month after his father's death. Christie confessed:

I didn't actually want to do it at first because

I thought I didn't know how to do Shakespeare. I do like challenges, but not situations of fear or uncertainty because I don't know what I'll get out of them. I have to want to do something. But my friends said, 'Oh, you must do it. Gertrude is one of those parts that you can't turn down.' And to do a film with Kenneth had a certain cachet. It's so specific, what he's doing, taking the Shakespeare canon, making it accessible to a new generation. I thought it would be an adventure.

Christie's performance was rightly praised, as she worked with a mix of the old and the new, from Gérard Depardieu, Charlton Heston, Jack Lemmon, Richard Attenborough, Brian Blessed, Richard Briers, Judi Dench, John Gielgud and John Mills to Billy Crystal, Rufus Sewell, Robin Williams and Kate Winslet. 'I wanted people to be excited by the event of this combination of people,' explained Branagh, 'to be intrigued by Robin Williams and Julie Christie being in a scene together. It lends a certain excitement. I've always believed Shakespeare is for everybody, so we cast it colour-blind, accent-blind and nationality-blind.' British comedian Ken Dodd even had a cameo role as Yorick.

Branagh, who played Hamlet, was impressed by Christie's interpretation of her role. 'Gertude, in Julie's view, has not had an adulterous affair with Claudius before the play begins and she doesn't know that he murdered her husband,' he said. 'That was important to her . . . And she's an incredibly beautiful woman who—in an underwritten but pivotal role, which Gertrude is—told me things about the Queen in a way that I'd never seen before.'

The film was a visual delight, only the third in twenty-five years to be shot in the extra-wide Panavision 70 mm format, after the Tom Cruise-Nicole Kidman American pioneers drama *Far and Away* in 1992 and director Bernardo Bertolucci's *Little Buddha* a year later, starring Keanu Reeves. In fact, the 70 mm format had been used throughout the 1950s and 1960s on epics such as *Oklahoma!*, *My Fair Lady*, *Around the World in 80 Days*, *Lawrence of Arabia*, *Cleopatra*, *Ben-Hur* and *Doctor Zhivago*.

Most of *Hamlet's* $9\frac{1}{2}$-week shoot, in early 1996, took place on five sound stages at Shepperton Studios, Middlesex. With much of the joint British-American production's action set in the main palace hall, Stages A and B were linked by a long corridor, with small sets such as Gertrude's rooms connected to the passageway.

Like Richard E. Grant in *Karaoke*, Branagh admitted to having 'admired and lusted after' Christie when he was young. During the filming, he spotted what is perhaps the secret of Christie's screen performance—she appears to remain unaware of the camera. He revealed that she was 'very nervous about doing this, very intimidated by Shakespeare' and added, 'Still strangely frightened on a film set. You'd say, "Julie, why don't you move a bit to your right." "Oh, where's the camera?" "What do you mean? It's over here." "Oh, I hadn't noticed it. I've been doing this for 30 years and I still can't get it right."'

Director of photography Alex Thomson, who had worked with Christie thirty years earlier as camera operator on *Fahrenheit 451*, recalled that she still harboured insecurities about her acting ability. 'In one scene, I was pointing out to Julie the importance of hitting a mark—a mark we make on the floor so that the actors can bring their toes to it for positioning purposes—which is important for the composition of the picture,' he said. 'I remember Julie saying, "I'm dreadful at marks. In all these years, I've never actually learned the technical bits of film."'

Before filming, Branagh took the cast through their paces in three weeks of rehearsing. 'We did things in rehearsal like running the entire play by candlelight one morning,' he said. 'All the immediate members of the crew were made to sit and watch it. Everybody was involved and knew what we were doing by watching us and a very nervous Julie Christie, who'd never been asked to do anything like this in her life before and had to be sedated when I told her. It was in order for the actors to experience where they were in the play emotionally when we shot out of order.'

Christie admitted, 'It was hard. I had no idea where I was supposed to be when. I had spatial dyslexia. I went and cried in the loo. But we all got through it. It was different from any other film I've ever made.' Yet another actor proved to be star-struck and slightly in awe of Christie. 'Billy Crystal could barely speak the day Julie Christie came on set,' revealed Branagh.

Despite her nerves while performing Shakespeare, Christie made a favourable impression on many people working on *Hamlet*. 'She was the life and soul, and the crew adored her,' recalled Richard Briers, who played Polonius. 'She got a bigger round of applause than I did at the end of the shoot. Julie is just such a sunny woman—great fun and enthusiastic. Also, she treated everybody as entirely equal. She had no snobbery or side to her at all.'

This latest screen version of *Hamlet* was also well received, measuring up well alongside Laurence Olivier's 1948 classic. In addition to good central performances and Alex Thomson's stunning photography, the picture was praised for production designer Tim Harvey's sumptuous sets and Alex Byrne's costumes, which were given a boost by

Branagh's decision to reset the story in the mid-to-late nineteenth century.

Following her roles in *Hamlet* and on stage in *Old Times*, Christie, after a lifetime of uncertainty about her own talents, began to believe in herself more. 'I didn't fall flat on my face doing *Old Times* and I also managed to push myself through *Hamlet* without falling,' she said. 'That quite surprised me. God knows whether I'm good or bad in it, but that's beside the point. I went to places where I haven't gone before—pushed away barriers that had existed for years.' The year 1996 proved to be a busy one for Christie. After making *Hamlet*, she travelled to Montreal, Canada, to shoot a film that cast her in the romantic lead once more and brought a third Oscar nomination, a quarter of a century after her previous one. The comedy-drama *Afterglow* was produced by Robert Altman and written and directed by Alan Rudolph, who had worked as an assistant director for Altman two decades earlier on a handful of films, including *Nashville.* Both had found it increasingly difficult to make the type of pictures they preferred, which explored people's relationships, although Rudolph's were less satirical.

Altman, who had directed Christie in *McCabe & Mrs Miller* and *Nashville*, was instrumental in persuading her and Nick Nolte to talk to the director about starring in *Afterglow.* Finding backing for the project was the producer-director partnership's hardest job, and they eventually worked with a budget of less than $6 million. 'On this film, we got started at the last minute, as always,' explained Rudolph, 'because of the financing and because Julie Christie had still not agreed to be in the film. That's always the case with my films, since they're so low-budget.'

Christie's star status was guaranteed with a contractual clause stating that her name would be 'above the title, in second position, separate card, in a size of type (and color of type) not less than that accorded Nolte. The stars played a married couple, handyman Lucky (Fix-It) Mann and faded B-movie actress Phyllis, who continues to watch videotapes of her dreadful, old pictures. Jonny Lee Miller and Lara Flynn Boyle acted ambitious businessman Jeffrey Byron and his broody, sexually frustrated young wife, Marianne. Both marriages are in trouble, for different reasons, the older Manns never having come to terms with their daughter's departure after hearing one of their bitter arguments, the Byrons simply not sharing the same aims in life. Both couples' lives become intertwined when Marianne becomes infatuated with Lucky and Jeffrey falls for Phyllis.

Unlike some directors with whom Christie had worked previously, most notably David Lean, Rudolph did not plan the specifics of scenes before shooting started. He preferred to react to the actors' actions and emotions, and often moved the camera from one to another in a scene instead of switching angles, which requires moving round the equipment and performing each scene more than once.

This more 'real' filming was used to greatest effect at the end of *Afterglow*, when Lucky walks up to the bedroom, finds Phyllis wailing on the bed and tries to comfort her. The camera moves round to show the open door and, down the stairs, a girl who could be the couple's long-lost daughter. The howling was Christie's idea and, according to Rudolph, it was so loud that some of the film crew put their hands over their ears. 'I couldn't wait for it to be over,' said the director, 'and then finally "Cut!" and I heard Julie say, "That was rather thrilling, wasn't it?" '

Afterglow premiered at the Cannes Film Festival, in May 1997. After seeing the film, Emmanuel Levy wrote in the Hollywood trade paper *Variety*, 'In a major comeback, the still strikingly beautiful Julie Christie renders such a captivating performance that she alone justifies the price of admission ... In her most polished performance since *Shampoo* and *Heaven Can Wait*, Christie dominates every scene she is in, rendering the witty, often wickedly funny lines that Rudolph has scripted for her with the kind of suave irony brought by experience and *savoir vivre*.'

'It's great to see Christie back on screen

again,' enthused Tom Shone in the *Sunday Times*, on the film's release in Britain exactly a year later, 'harder to see what persuaded her to return. It couldn't have been the script . . . As it progresses, though, Christie loosens the script's lockjaw into something more feline and relaxed.' The performance was enough to earn Christie an Oscar nomination as Best Actress, alongside fellow-Brits Judi Dench, Helena Bonham Carter and Kate Winslet. In the event, the award went to American Helen Hunt for her performance in *As Good As It Gets* on Oscars night, in April 1998, a month before *Afterglow* was even released in Britain.

The British press showed great interest in what their actresses were wearing to the ceremony. Christie had been for fittings with John Galliano but made a last-minute switch to New York lace and beading experts Badgley Mischka to don a silver spiderweb, crystal-beaded lace dress. 'If Oscar night was a competition of style, Christie, 58, won hands down,' declared the *Independent*.

Christie subsequently confessed to having been baffled by the meaning of *Afterglow* and bemused by the Oscar nomination. 'I like Alan Rudolph's work, but couldn't understand the film,' she explained. 'I've done many I can't understand. I was surprised to be nominated and thought I'd better analyse what it's all about. Now I know: me not being dead was one factor. People are glad you're still able to

285

function. I couldn't relate to the part, except for a sort of dourness and also she's funny. I'm not often given funny parts. People think I'm romantic.'

Before the Oscars ceremony, Christie had rebuffed speculation that her nomination marked a permanent return to film-making for her. 'I wasn't going to do the film, because I am not into making films,' she insisted. 'I probably won't do any more. That's not my plan.' At the same time, it was public knowledge that Christie had succumbed to the temptation to make herself look younger by having a minor facelift. Christie had said eleven years earlier:

> The loss of beauty does worry me. If you have lived with a face all your life, it is hard as the face changes and your mind isn't changing at the same pace as your body. I think it is awfully difficult when change happens and you are not controlling it. Actresses notice the face so much you have to look at yourself in the mirror and be hard on yourself and deal with what you choose to show and not to show. Actresses are like surgeons in the way they look at themselves. They have to be: their face is part of their tools.

Now Christie said she had to balance this feeling against her worry that plastic surgery was something that separated the 'haves' from the 'have-nots', another form of consumerism— 'irresistible and very, very sad'. Eventually, she made the decision simply to modify her jawline. 'I had all these double chins and I thought, oh, can't bear that,' she explained. 'My jawline isn't exactly the same as the jawline I was born with. I will try and resist the big stuff, I think. But it's hard. It's very hard going to America, where people who are older than you appear to be younger. That is really, really undermining. You know they're older than you, and you look like their mother.'

But it came as a shock to Christie that the revelation that she had undergone surgery should generate so much publicity and comment. 'It was a tiny thing, far less than has been made out, done for professional reasons,' she insisted. 'I should have said nothing—it's an irrelevance. You can't tell the truth because it becomes a feast for hyenas to tear you apart.'

Deciding on plastic surgery had little to do with recreating the enigmatic beauty that made her an icon of the 1960s. For Christie, the past held no fascination. 'I don't yearn for the past,' she explained after her Oscar nomination for *Afterglow*, 'or long for it, or remember it in any real way, because it isn't real. It's over with. It's finished. It's gone.'

She was happy with the present and looked forward to the future. 'I have a partner whom I love very much, so I am not actually alone,' said Christie back in the late 1980s. 'But, at the same time, I am on my own quite a bit because he lives in London and I am in Wales . . . At one time I thought I would be completely alone. Towards the end of the Hollywood period and coming back here, I thought I would grow old alone. I had not thought then that I would be with someone until I died. But it didn't fill me with fear at all. I adore my own company. I love being alone.'

In 1999 Campbell, who had been working on the *Guardian* for the previous nine years as a crime reporter, moved to Los Angeles as a correspondent for the paper. Shortly afterwards, in September of that year, he helped Christie to move into a house that she had bought at Ojai, about seventy-five miles outside Los Angeles. It gave her a base if she were tempted by another Hollywood picture, although there was no indication that she would act again. In the three years after making *Afterglow*, Christie's only involvement in films was to lend her voice to *The Miracle Maker*, an animated feature about the life of Jesus, and to join television newscaster Julia Somerville in introducing the short *Different Strokes—The Film*, made for a charity that helps stroke victims.

But buying a house in the United States also offered Christie the chance to get geographically closer to her declared dream of 'sitting by the Pacific in Mexico, watching the sea for ever'. Contemplating old age, Christie added, 'I worry about becoming really ill and not being able to move or carry my shopping. Unless you have servants in this day and age it is quite difficult getting old. If I have to be in one spot, at least if it's the Pacific I can look at something beautiful. I think I'm realistic. Maybe I'm not . . .'

APPENDICES

Films

Each film title is followed by alternative titles, the role played by Julie Christie, the production company and year appearing on the copyright line of the film, the director and country of origin.

Crooks Anonymous, Babette (Independent Artists, 1962). Dir: Ken Annakin, *GB*.

The Fast Lady, Claire Chingford (Independent Artists, 1962). Dir: Ken Annakin, *GB*.

Billy Liar!, Liz (Vic Films/Waterhall, 1963). Dir: John Schlesinger, *GB*.

Young Cassidy, Daisy Battles (Sextant Films, 1964). Dir: John Ford/Jack Cardiff, *GB*.

Darling, Diana Scott (Vic Films/Appia Films, 1965). Dir: John Schlesinger, *GB*.

Zhivago: Behind the Camera with David Lean (documentary short on the filming of *Doctor Zhivago*) (Thomas Craven Film Corporation, 1965). Dir: Thomas Craven, US.

Doctor Zhivago, Lara (MGM, 1965). Dir: David Lean, *GB/US*.

Fahrenheit 451, Linda/Clarisse (Anglo-Enterprise Film Productions, 1966). Dir: François Truffaut, *GB*.

Star (documentary short), Herself (subject of film) (Alan Lovell, 1966). Dir: Alan Lovell, *GB*.

Far from the Madding Crowd, Bathsheba (Appia Films/Vic Films, 1967). Dir: John Schlesinger, *GB*.

Tonite Let's All Make Love in London (documentary), Herself (Lorrimer Films, 1967). Dir: Peter Whitehead, *GB*.

Petulia, Petulia Danner (Petersham Films, 1968). Dir: Richard Lester, *US*.

In Search of Gregory (also titled *Alla Ricerde Gregory*), Catherine Morelli (Vic Films/Vera Films, 1968). Dir: Peter Wood, *GB-Italy*.

The Games, Uncredited (Linsk/Twentieth Century-Fox, 1969). Dir: Michael Winner, *GB*.

The Go-Between, Marian Maudsley (Associated British Productions, 1970). Dir: Joseph Losey, *GB*.

McCabe & Mrs Miller, Constance Miller (Warner Brothers, 1971). Dir: Robert Altman, US.

'Don't Look Now', Laura Baxter (DLN Ventures Partnership, 1973). Dir: Nicolas Roeg, *GB-Italy*.

Shampoo, Jackie Shawn (Persky-Bright, 1975). Dir: Hal Ashby, US.

Nashville, Herself (ABC, 1975). Dir: Robert Altman, US.

Demon Seed, Dr Susan Harris (MGM, 1977). Dir: Donald Cammell, *US*.

Heaven Can Wait, Betty Logan (Shelburne Associates, 1978). Dir: Warren Beatty/Buck Henry, US.

Memoirs of a Survivor, 'D' (Memorial Enterprises, 1981). Dir: David Gladwell, *GB*.

The Animals Film (documentary), Narrator (Slick Picks International, 1981). Dir: Victor Schonfeld, *GB-US*.

Les Quarantièmes Rugissants (The Roaring Forties), Catherine Dantec (Cinema 7, 1981). Dir: Christian de Chalonge, *France*.

The Return of the Soldier, Kitty Baldry (Brent Walker Film Productions, 1982). Dir: Alan Bridges, *GB*.

Heat and Dust, Anne (1980s; in Satipur Town) (Merchant Ivory Productions, 1982). Dir: James Ivory, *GB*.

The Gold Diggers, Ruby (British Film Institute Production Board, 1983). Dir: Sally Potter, *GB*.

Power, Ellen Freeman (Lorimar, 1985). Dir: Sidney Lumet, *US*.

Miss Mary, Miss Mary Mulligan (GEA Cinematografica, 1986). Dir: Maria Luisa Bemberg, *Argentina-US*.

La Mémoire Tatouée (also titled *Secret Obsession*, *Silent Memory*, *Champagne Amer* and *Tattooed Memory*), Betty (Paris Pro-Motion, 1986). Dir: Ridha Béhi, *France-Tunisia*.

Agent Orange—Policy of Poison

(documentary), Narrator (Activision Video, 1987). Dir: Rod Iverson, *GB*.

Fools of Fortune, Mrs Quinton (PolyGram Filmed Entertainment, 1990). Dir: Pat O'Connor, *Ireland*.

Dragonheart, Aislinn (Universal Pictures, 1996). Dir: Rob Cohen, *US*.

Hamlet, Gertrude (Castle Rock Entertainment, 1996). Dir: Kenneth Branagh, *US-GB*.

Afterglow, Phyllis Mann (Afterglow, 1997). Dir: Alan Rudolph, *US*.

Different Strokes—The Film (documentary short), Introduction (Annex Films, 1999). Dir: Clive Jackson, *GB*.

The Miracle Maker, Voice of Rachel (Sianel Pedwar Cymru/Christmas Films, 1999). Dir: Stanislav Sokolov/Derek Hayes, *GB-Russia*.

Television

Each programme title is followed by alternative titles, the role played by Julie Christie, the production company and year appearing on the copyright line of the programme, and the first British transmission details showing channel and date.

Call Oxbridge 2000, Ann (ATV, one episode, 1961). *ITV, 8 October 1961.*

A for Andromeda, Christine/Andromeda (serial) (BBC, 1961). *BBC, 10, 17, 24, 31*

October, 7, 14 November 1961.

Dangerous Corner ('Play of the Week'), Betty Whitehead (Granada Television, 1963). *ITV 19 March 1963.*

The Saint (Episode: *Judith*), Judith (ATV/ITC, 1963). *ITV, 3 October 1963.*

Separate Tables, Anne Shank/Sybil Railton-Bell (HTV/Ely and Evie Landau, 1983). *ITV, 2 January 1984.*

An Evening for Nicaragua, Participant (Ibt Productions, 1983). *Channel Four, 1 September 1983.*

Why Their News is Bad News ('Open Door'), Presenter (BBC, 1984). *BBC2, 23 February 1984.*

Vater and Sohne (also titled *Fathers and Sons* and *Sins of the Fathers)* (mini-series), Charlotte Deutz (Bavaria Atelier, Germany, 1986). *BBC, 12 November 1986.*

Dadah Is Death (also titled *A Long Way From Home*, *A Long Way Home* and *Deadly Decision),* Barbara Barlow (mini-series) (Home Productions, Australia-US, 1988). *BBC, 30 January 1988.*

Prisoners of Conscience, Presenter (BBC, 1992). *BBC2, 8 December 1992.*

The Railway Station Man, Helen Cuffe (TVM) (BBC Films/Turner Pictures, 1992). *BBC2, 30 December 1993* ('Screen Two').

Karaoke, Lady Ruth Balmer (two episodes in four-part serial) (Whistling Gypsy Production, 1996). *BBC1/Channel Four, 5/6,*

19/20 May 1996 (each episode screened on BBC1 and repeated a day later on Channel Four).

The Readiness is All: The Filming of Hamlet (documentary on the making of the film *Hamlet*) (BBC Education, 1997). *BBC2, 15 February 1997.*

As Narrator

Taking on the Bomb ('Broadside') (documentary) (Broadside Productions, 1983). *Channel Four, 5 January 1983.*

Yilmaz Güney: His Life, His Films (documentary) (Try Again/Jane Balfour Films, 1987). *Channel Four, 21 January 1987.*

Katie and Eilish: Siamese Twins ('First Tuesday') (documentary) (Yorkshire Television, 1992). *ITV, 4 August 1992.*

For Better For Worse ('Life Stories') (BBC, 1994). *BBC1, 3 May 1994.*

Death and Beauty ('The Slate') (drama-documentary) (BBC Wales, 1994). *BBC2, 22 July 1994.*

Small Miracles ('Network First') (documentary) (Yorkshire Television, 1995). *ITV, 4 April 1995.*

Eilish: Life Without Katie ('Network First') (documentary) (Yorkshire Television, 1995). *ITV 29 August 1995.*

Chosen People (documentary) (Caledonia,

Sterne & Wyld, 2000). *BBC2, 3 January 2000.*

As Interviewee/Contributor

Moviemen!: David Lean, Interviewee (Thames Television, 1970). *ITV, 17 March 1970.*

Aspel & Company, Interviewee, publicizing Oxfam Cambodia film (LWT, 1988). *ITV, 24 September 1988.*

This Week: The Last Picture Show?, Interviewee in current affairs programme comparing the British and French film industries (Thames Television, 1990). *ITV, 5 July 1990.*

Hollywood UK: British Cinema in the 60s (three episodes in five-part series), Interviewee (BBC, 1993). *BBC2, 5, 12, 26 September 1993.*

Close Up, Contributor, choosing clip from the film *Urga* (BBC, 1995). *BBC2, 9 November 1995.*

François Truffaut: The Man Who Loved Cinema (two-part documentary), Interviewee (BBC, 1996). *BBC2, 9, 16 March 1996.*

Kiss Kiss Bang Bang, Contributor, choosing one of her favourite films, *Fear Eats the Soul* (Mentorn Barraclough Carey, 1998). *Channel Four, 10 November 1998.*

Theatre

Frinton Summer Theatre repertory company (1960, 1961).
Birmingham Repertory Company June to December 1963):
The Country Wife, Alithea
Thark, Kitty Stratton
The Good Person of Szechwan, Sister-in-Law (The Family of Eight)
Next Time I'll Sing to You, Lizzie
Colombe, A Chiropodist
Between These Four Walls (revue), Various roles
The Comedy of Errors, Luciana (Royal Shakespeare Company) (Aldwych Theatre, London, plus Eastern Europe tour, North America tour and command performance at Windsor Castle, 1964).
Uncle Vanya, Elena (Circle in the Square—Joseph E. Levine Theatre, New York, 1973).
Old Times, Kate (Wyndham's Theatre, 1995).
Suzanna Andler, Suzanna Andler (Minerva Studio, Chichester, 1997).

Awards

Society of Film & Television Arts Best Actress Award for *Billy Liar!* (1963).
Best Actress Academy Award for *Darling* (1965).

Society of Film & Television Arts Best Actress Award for *Darling* (1965).
New York Film Critics Best Actress Award for *Darling* (1965).
Variety Club of Great Britain Best Actress for *Darling* (1965).
National American Board of Review Best Actress award for *Darling* (1965).
Donatello Award for *Doctor Zhivago* (1965).
Society of Film & Television Arts Best Actress Award for *Fahrenheit 451* (1966).
Best Dramatic Actress Motion Picture Laurel Award (1967).
Herald Award (1967).
British Academy of Film & Television Arts Fellowship (1997).
Evening Standard British Film Awards Best Actress for *Afterglow* (1997).

Nominations

Best Actress Oscar nomination for *McCabe & Mrs Miller* (1971).
Best Actress Oscar nomination for *Afterglow* (1997).